(S)KINFOLK:
Chimamanda Ngozi Adichie's *Americanah*

Tochi Onyebuchi

FICTION ADVOCATE

New York • San Francisco • Providence

A Fiction Advocate Book

(S)kinfolk:
Chimamanda Ngozi's *Americanah*
© 2021 by Tochi Onyebuchi
All Rights Reserved

ISBN: 978-0-9994316-9-6

Interior design and composition, Greg Johnson, Textbook Perfect

FICTION ADVOCATE
New York • San Francisco • Providence
fictionadvocate.com

Published in the United States of America

To Jon Pitts-Wiley,
for the piano lessons

CONTENTS

INTRODUCTION

I remember only shouting, as though, with Nigerian gatherings, there never exists—never has and never will—any quiet. Cacophony attends house-cleaning, clamor seasons food prep. Every time cousins visited, I would hear my mother before I would see her. "Wake up, the Udehs are coming." "Wake up, the Nwachukus are coming." "Wake up, now! The Nwankwos are coming." And I would peel my cheek from my pillow, maybe brush my teeth and shower, maybe not, put on some sweats, and proceed to try as much as possible this early in the morning not to be useless.

Grease sizzles and pops. Mom is frying her plantains. The vacuum roars over carpet and growls when thrust under couches and tables. When I was younger, my siblings would amble around the house, completing their assigned tasks: sweeping and vacuuming the stairs, taking out the trash, wiping down the tables, rearranging furniture, bringing high-backed chairs out of the dining room to the living room. And later, setting up the speaker Mom had bought so that, when my cousin Nnamdi arrived, he could connect his Spotify and play Afrobeat for us and older Nigerian songs for the elders.

The first arrivals key up the noise as soon as they cross the threshold. By evening, the house is filled with lovely dissonance: the kids downstairs on my brother's Xbox, the grownups in the living room with their plates, arguing Nigerian politics beneath family portraits hung on the wall. A poster of Barack Obama in 2008 hangs above someone's head. With his arms folded, he levels a toothy grin over the assemblage, as though to say "this, too, is America."

We weren't the white heartland voters he fought so hard to win, we highly educated African immigrants and their over-educated progeny. It was assumed we would vote for him. Sure, he was Black. But he was also a double Ivy.

Eight years later, cousins have gathered for Thanksgiving. We've traded hosting duties every year with the Udehs, cousins in the Nigerian sense; or, rather, the immigrant sense. Anyone who was a close enough friend of my parents was an Uncle or an Aunt, their children my cousins, some of whom I didn't discover I did not share blood with until I was well into my 20s. In the '70s and '80s, the first of us arrived from Nigeria on student visas and set up a landing pad in the Northeast. Some settled in New York while others recreated as much of the homeland as they could in Massachusetts and, later, Connecticut, managing that immigrant duality of maintaining cultural memory and simultaneously accumulating the Promised Land's habits and customs. My father, questing after jobs and more education, was friends with Uncle Steve. Through him, he met my mother. In a few years, I, the first of four, would be born.

Nowhere was this immigrant duality more evident than at Thanksgiving, where gari and pepper soup sat in bowls alongside stuffing. Where jollof rice and fried rice and fried plantains surrounded the large turkey into which the designated "man of the house" was obligated to make the first cut. My father's death, just as I hovered on the cliff's edge of childhood, pushed me past adolescence and into the faux adulthood occupied by children who bear responsibilities ill-suited for their thin shoulders. From too early an age, I held the knife.

My mother's accent would thicken when family was near, especially after the arrival of my cousin Nnamdi, who, after coming to the US for college, earned his PhD at 23, then made a home for himself on the West Coast working in biomedical consulting. He ate the food Mom loved and loved to cook. He spoke in her idioms. He understood her Igbo and tossed it back to her, two tennis pros exchanging volleys and delighting in it. Envy was inevitable. I was jealous of their closeness, that he held so much of my mother's country in him, the intensity with which their tuning forks vibrated when they were in proximity. Mom laughed so loudly when they talked.

By 2016, my mother had assimilated as much as she was going to. She watched episodes of *Criminal Minds* before bed, then as US politics grew more visibly virulent and coarse, MSNBC, where she found what she considered reasoned analysis and considered outrage. Her English was near-impeccable, though her pronunciation of certain words betrayed foreign origins. I was never embarrassed when she said *embarASS*.

We had been following the election and its interminable leadup closely. Conversations between Mom and her four adult kids held a frankness and sophistication I could never imagine in the families of my friends. Among ourselves, we could speak caustically of the lower-class white Americans so eager to ride the Ford F-150s of white supremacy into their own extinction. I was so proud of her, this woman who castigated those whites who needed access to affordable healthcare the most and who so gleefully cheered for the man who unabashedly pledged to take it away from them, this woman who saw early on the power and hypocrisy of white evangelicals and perceived in them an influence that eluded most cable-news talking heads, this woman who saw in Donald J. Trump the endpoint of the race resentment that had been boiling in Americans since well before the passage of the Civil Rights Act.

By now, we had all finished college and brought home with us what we had learned, in class and outside of it. And I could exchange volleys with Mom. They weren't arguments, they were affirmations. She would say, regarding lower-class whites, "we are taking medicine for their headache," and I would laugh. My envy of cousin Nnamdi vanished.

Thanksgiving of 2016, the house obstreperous with three and a half families of Nigerians and an assortment of Mom's American friends, bore none of the pall I imagined in those households shocked into sorrow by Hillary Clinton's defeat. We knew what had happened, we expected it, and we expected those who had sown the seeds of their own destruction to quickly sink into buyer's remorse.

The conversation moved to American politics. I ran from wherever I had been in the house to the kitchen like a wrestler tagged into the fight, vaulting over the ropes to land a titanic elbow drop.

A few Uncles were present. Something was amiss. Their posture wasn't triumphalist, their shoulders were hunched defensively, their elbows at their sides while they gestured with their hands. And Mom and Aunty Liz were shouting while my younger sisters watched.

"I think you are being too hard on this Trump," Uncle Steve said. "I mean, let's see how it goes."

Before he could finish, Mom and Aunty Liz tag-teamed him with questions he was never meant to answer: "And what he has said about Mexicans?" "So you approve of the Muslim ban?" "Ah, so let him take away healthcare so people can die, then?" "He is a disgusting man, he does not even know where Syria is, and you approve?"

Then my youngest sister: "You didn't vote for him, did you?"

Uncle Steve's pause cratered the floor beneath us.

"But what about her emails?" Uncle Kenny chimed in. "You cannot trust a woman like that. She would have been under investigation."

Once Mom and Aunty Liz recovered their breath, the shouting reached a fever pitch.

My cousin Nnamdi lobbed his own grenades. "You talk of investigation when this man is as corrupt, if not more, than any Naija politician. You think, just because he has not mentioned you, that he will not come for you?"

"This is the worst thing to happen to gay rights," my youngest sister lamented. "People are going to die, Uncle. How could you?"

We laughed at my Uncles, but the hurt in my sister's voice was unmistakable. It hummed beneath each word.

We all felt betrayed. We were not a clan of hood-winked white Americans. We weren't vengeful racists rejoicing in the advent of our mendacious messiah. We were immigrants and their children. Amid the bludgeoning my Uncles endured, Nnamdi, smirking, said, "See? You should not have paid for us to go to such good schools." They were doing well. They worked in insurance and finance. They were solidly upper-middle class. They lived in multi-story houses in West Hartford. They were darker than me. And yet.

Among the epiphanies that attended this revelation was the fact that we were separate. Not I from my uncles, but us from African Americans. Looking at the vote totals afterwards, I noted with worry and confusion the small percentage of Blacks, mostly Black males, who had voted for the Republican. Why? Maybe because the myth of the self-made multi-millionaire figured so prominently in rap lyrics. But my Uncles detested rap and sneered whenever their American-born children blasted it in their cars. Maybe it was the bluster, the masculine posturing, the way he bulldozed through competition and juggernauted through opposition. But they were too smart and savvy to be fooled by that, weren't they? Maybe it was because they truly didn't trust the Democratic candidate to advocate for their interests. Maybe they saw in the attacks on her character some element of truth, that she was too cunning a political operator, that she changed positions too often, even when her switch was from "wrong" to "right." But surely they saw her qualifications. Maybe it was because the conservative misogyny they took with them from the Old Country had not been eroded by siring daughters and wishing them professional success.

Or maybe they believed themselves insulated. They believed their children insulated. When he vilified Black Americans, surely Trump didn't mean us who had contributed so much in taxes to American greatness, us who had graduated from august educational institutions, us who had walked the halls of power, us who had befriended future mayors and Senators, us who had CEOs in our Rolodexes. This country had wounded us, sure. But we had not been born within the orbit of African-American suffering. My Uncles survived Jim Crow by having grown up in a different country altogether. If they knew of the Detroit Race Riots, it was simply as a historical fact, and a fleeting one at that. A curiosity.

And I came from them.

For the majority of my life, I'd believed myself Black exactly like African Americans. Just as much as them, I was a potential hashtag to be propelled into brief online popularity by a police officer's bullet. Just like them, I'd lost out on jobs and romantic relationships because of unvoiced prejudice.

Wasn't I Black like them?

The more I thought about my Uncles, the more the question morphed into "Had I ever been". Was their experience mine to claim?

I was African, my genealogy traced straight back to the African Continent. And I was American, born a citizen. Yet that adjectival hyphen. That hyphen that carried with it so much American history, that hyphen that was evidence of America's Original Sin, evidence

TOCHI ONYEBUCHI

of the bill the country had run up against so large a swath of its population. Strive as I might to know and understand, if you cut through the noise of the older generation's argument, if you slice through the clamor of immigrants celebrating American holidays, in the silence, a single realization waits.

I was not African-American.

PART 1

SOMETHING SO WHITE

Second Sight

I did not see myself in a novel until I was 26 years old.

In 2014, as part of a book club started with some law school friends in the early throes of life at corporate firms, we selected *Americanah*, Chimamanda Ngozi Adichie's third novel.

It's a love story about two Nigerians—one of whom emigrates to America and one of whom tries to make a go of it in London—inextricably linked by their love for each other. I found it an incredible book. An immigrant story of immense empathetic depth, it also scathingly and incisively cuts into race, racism, and racialism in the US. Not just degrees of Blackness but even the titanically flawed ways in which professed liberal whites relate to both African Americans and American Africans. The main character, willful, perceptive Ifemelu, peppers the novel with entries from her blog. Contained in the entries are her observations on white Americans and their relationship with Blackness. Indeed, it sometimes reads like an instruction manual for those in her position: emigrés from Africa to this new, confusing, confused country. Learn to take offense when white Americans make disparaging references to watermelon, even though you personally may enjoy watermelon. Learn that "racist" is the worst thing you could call a white person, because those poor people cannot bring themselves to take any responsibility for the horrors historically visited on people who look like you. Learn of the hierarchies of whiteness and that Jewish is white but not quite. Learn that some Jews will try to engage in what is called the "Oppression Olympics." Learn that so much of Barack Obama's appeal stems from the fact that he married a woman darker than him.

The novel sprawls and contains industrial amounts of pathos.

It is also, in almost every way, the story of my family. My cousins, my mother, myself. It is the story of Americanization: contentious but enduring relations with family back home, the upheaval of expectations upon arrival in the Promised Land, the anxieties that attend the return home. All the ways America, simply by being America, crushes Nigerian-ness, and how Nigerian-ness manages to persist in the face of it. The massive divide between African Americans and American Africans, the class issues, the problems that persistently plague Nigeria, the pesky ardor that expats and those American-born and England-born Nigerians have for their home country. All of it is here in abundance, glorious and incandescent.

Books, to me, are evanescent exercises in empathy. The splitting of consciousness that, for the duration of that reading, tells you "be Bigger Thomas," "be Katniss Everdeen," "be Quentin Compson," "be Emma Bovary," "be Jean Valjean," "be Tom Sawyer," "be Janie Crawford," "be George Smiley," "be Rand al-Thor," and be yourself also.

Reading *Americanah*, I was captured by alien sensations. From the maid in an early anecdote not getting hired because Kosi is too jealous to have any speck of compassion, to the reporter's despair at Chief's party where all he sees is pasta and cold cuts and no Nigerian food, to Kosi saying "We thank God" as a response to everything, to the whole first scene about hair (my poor sisters!), to characters named Nneoma and Chijioke...

Recognition.

Recognition in a piece of fiction can go soul-deep. This character loves as obsessively as I do. That character's anguish explains my own. This character wears his blue collar as proudly as I wear mine. That character is confused by the idea of children he does not know whether or not he wants, just like I am. This character's love of winter perplexes his or her friends just as much as my love of winter perplexes mine. That character endures the same trials and tribulations working her hair as my sisters do (again, my poor sisters!). That character has a mother who prays with the same fervent, expansive verve that fills my own mother's entreaties. That character has uncles and aunts with an inexplicable fondness for Guinness, just like me.

So accurate and so meticulous were its depictions of life as a Nigerian and as a Nigerian in America that I found myself transported not only to my own youth but, through a miracle of translocation, into what life might have been like for my mother, who arrived in America in the early 1980s.

She came for school, as so many of her generation did, and settled at Liberty University in Lynchburg, VA. When asked why there, of all places—a school that, in my mind, existed as a hotbed of hostility to the very notion of diversity—she says simply that "it was a good Christian school."

The immigrant seeks out the familiar, or, in the alternative, constructs it themselves. Raised as a Christian, Christians were familiar, went the thinking. God had guided her all her life. It makes sense that she would seek Him out upon arriving on foreign shores.

Ecclesiastic Education

My mother's Christianity is a union between the white missionaries' *mission civilatrice* and local animist traditions. It is a faith that takes the Bible both seriously and literally, that sees in demon possession not a metaphor for schizophrenia or bipolar disorder but the actual Devil taking actual hold of a human being's form. The story of Legion isn't a parable of mental illness. It is simply the story of Legion. Hers is a faith that will have penitents calling on local healers and village elders to, quite literally, cast the Devil out. "You there, you shouldn't be practicing magic," says the colonizer, "but I have a sore throat and could you bless it for me, please?"

My mother prays with the fervor of someone for whom every step on American soil is sacrosanct. As though she has just now arrived and cannot believe her good fortune. It is prayer pregnant with thanks, gravid with gratitude. It is prayer that enlists the entire body. It is an immigrant's prayer, neither white nor Black, but more recognizably Black than white. It is an ideal to which I've aspired, because it has always sounded right. Not the hollow entreaty of a wordsmith, but the steamrolling of a true penitent. In those moments, as a child, when I would peek at her with one eye, she would glow with otherworldly power radiating from her bones. She was a superhero the way she raised us, and when I watched her pray, I felt I had chanced a glimpse at the sun from which she derived her powers.

Knowing this about her makes it easier to see, given the selectivity with which information flowed from West to East in the 1980s, why she saw in Liberty University, the largest Evangelical Christian university in the world, a place for her to set up shop.

It is easy to believe that a time when people traveled without the Internet was some paleolithic period of guessing and, more often than not, guessing wrong; of leaping and landing somewhere unexpected; of missing the mark. In some ways, this was Mom's experience. The bits and pieces of America that had reached her beforehand, filtered through the sieve of cultural imperialism, consisted mostly of Michael Jackson tapes and episodes of *Dynasty*. America is not Texas, despite what many Texans would have people believe, and I can only imagine her shock—a residue of it left in her voice when she tells me later on—at landing in JFK on her way to Bradley and seeing her first overweight American. "I thought they all looked like *Dynasty*." Nary a ten-gallon hat in sight. Instead, through the doors, she could see white on the ground outside and sun shining so bright as to nearly blind her. She and a relative stood by the doors to their terminal, watching in wonder. Her first sight of real snow. The door opens. A gust blasts through. Mom emits a cry and scurries away, shocked that something so bright, something so white, could be so cold. If only she had packed a coat.

She arrives at Liberty and boards with an Ethiopian woman. They study by candlelight and attend chapel together. And Mom tells me, bemused, about the white people who asked—apparently with genuine curiosity— whether or not she had a tail. "Yes," my mother would tell them. Sometimes, she would continue with "but I had it shortened when I was little" or "it only grows at night." I imagine her intelligence spilling out of the classroom into a playful wit. I like to imagine that she smiled quite a bit.

She doesn't talk much about the racism she experienced at Liberty. While she was there, Jesse Jackson became the first Black man to speak on their campus, as she tells it. She witnessed a student population and a faculty and administration in the thrall of Reagan, a "majority of people, regarded as favoring firm moral standards." I don't think anyone there at that time would have taken umbrage at what the Oxford English Dictionary said of the Moral Majority movement growing on campus. It was Jerry Falwell's fiefdom, and when she speaks of Liberty, it is less as a school than as a kingdom, a dominion designed in the image of the Southern Baptist.

It was a place that saw the Bible, particularly its Old Testament, much the same way Originalist jurists view the Constitution's base text. Which is to say that this blessed thing becomes, in their hands, a tool for the execution of a pernicious and myopic worldview.

Mom likes to tell the story of how her Ethiopian friend was always running late for chapel. Her friend would ask her to "save me a seat, please" because the hall would often fill to capacity within minutes. And Mom would assure her friend that there would be a seat waiting for her. She would find a place in a pew, a single Black face among the white congregation, and almost immediately, the white congregants would squeeze into another pew. There was always a seat waiting for my mother's friend.

As she tells it now, whatever confusion she experienced carried no hurt. She never seemed to ask "why won't they sit with me". Instead, she realized that their backwardness could be turned to her advantage. Their racism was less a thing that impeded her rise than it was a thing that forced white people into increasingly painful mental, rhetorical, and situational contortions. She saw in their malice only a baffling quirk.

In *The Souls of Black Folk*, DuBois talks of the first time he saw himself seen as Black. A young white classmate refuses his gift perfunctorily while the others in the class exchange their cards happily:

> I remember well when the shadow swept across me. I was a little thing, away up in the hills of New England, where the dark Housatonic winds between Hoosac and Taghkanic to the sea. In a wee wooden schoolhouse, something put it into the boys' and girls' heads to buy gorgeous visiting-cards—ten cents a package—and exchange. The exchange was merry, till one girl, a tall newcomer, refused my card—refused it peremptorily, with a glance.

Then it dawned upon me with a certain sudden-
ness that I was different from the others; or like,
mayhap, in heart and life and longing, but shut out
from their world by a vast veil. I had thereafter no
desire to tear down that veil, to creep through; I
held all beyond it in common contempt, and lived
above it in a region of blue sky and great wandering
shadows. That sky was bluest when I could beat
my mates at examination-time, or beat them at a
foot-race, or even beat their stringy heads. Alas,
with the years all this fine contempt began to fade;
for the words I longed for, and all their dazzling
opportunities, were theirs, not mine.[1]

He writes of what episodes like this did to others
like him, how it closed them off or crippled them. He
writes of the prison it made for them, "walls strait and
stubborn to the whitest, but relentlessly narrow, tall,
and unscalable to sons of night who must plod darkly
on in resignation, or beat unavailing palms against the
stone, or steadily, half hopelessly, watch the streak of
blue above."[2]

Caribbean historian and theorist Elsa Goveia calls
for precisely this sort of analysis to combat the popular
forgetting that plagued the region post-independence.

But for her, it was not enough to see oppressor and oppressed in a neat and clearly delineated binary. It was necessary

> to grasp in all its complexity the nature of the influence which slavery has exercised over their history. But they will not be able to do this until they can see the white colonists, the free people of colour, and the Negro slaves as joint participants in a human situation which shaped all their lives... Good intentions are not enough, and the road to hell is paved with authoritative half-truths. No one is ever liberated from the past by being taught how easy it is to substitute new shibboleths for old.[3]

She implicates slavers, the enslaved, and the free in a miasma of caste and race at the center of which lies chattel slavery, but whose wheel spokes extend far in every direction, beyond the contours of colonial history and European history to, in her vision, create a unique and fully-formed historical context for the West Indies. The project here, based on the premise that knowledge is power, is to free the Caribbean from being, as Guyanese novelist Wilson Harris once put it, "embalmed in his deprivations—embalmed as a derivative tool-making, fence-making animal."[4] An individual liberation coincidental with the awakening of a larger geo-temporal consciousness. An elaboration of the body schema such that the stretching out of an arm to reach for matches and light a cigarette exists outside the white gaze, ceases to be a thing experienced in the third person and becomes, instead, a first-person event.

Captured here is so much of the plight of what W.E.B. DuBois calls the American Negro, for whom slavery is the Original Sin, the "sum of all villainies,"[5] and for whom Emancipation was "the key to a promised land of sweeter beauty than ever stretched before the eyes of wearied Israelites."[6]

The students and faculty and administration at the Liberty University my mother attended might take umbrage with DuBois's appropriation of Scripture. The Bible had, in fact, been used to countenance slavery. It had been weaponized in the service of Jim Crow. Equating African Americans with the Israelites begged the question: who, then, were the Egyptians who had enslaved them?

Did Mom ask that question when learning her catechisms? What was it like to be a congregant of color in a "default" church, a church that marches to the doctrinal drumroll as opposed to a church whose spirit sways to the dirge of shared tragedy? Doctrine is not meant to have a color. Faith is heaven and earth; it is night-time stars guiding slaves, and it is the turned earth of a freshly-dug grave; it is the wafer and the wine; it is the lightning that strikes on the road to Damascus, and it is blinking sweat out of your eyes as you work the field. It is getting on a plane to make a future for yourself in a country you've never been to. It is the history in the air we breathe, and it is the history in the earth on which we stand. It is a baby born. It is the dying of the light.

But Mom was not descended from slaves, so this was never her calculus to solve.

Her genre of interaction with white people was primarily observation, which is why I thought of her when reading of Ifemelu.

Ifemelu begins *Americanah* in Princeton on her way to the nail salon. During the journey she thinks of the white people she encounters, carried away at the sight of them to the blog she has, at this point in the novel, quit writing. Caustic and incisive, she betrays a learned omniscience: the dreadlocked white dude, his shirt tattered and his hair like "old twine ropes," tries to convince her that he is a social justice warrior but ranks class higher than race in the vectors of oppression that need battling; then there is the white middle manager on a flight who tells her of his adopting a Black baby, saying with perhaps a bit of lamentation that "[n]obody wants black babies in this country, and I don't mean biracial. I mean black."[7]

The blog posts peppered throughout the book reveal a curing process of the bafflement that strikes Ifemelu at the behavior of white people, the ways that their role in American racism and their whiteness have pretzeled them into increasingly complex psychological contortions.

But she pines for the homeland. Nigeria is where she came from. It crafted her bones, it mixed together the plasma in her blood, it creased every wrinkle in her brain. And Blaine, her African-American partner for three years, is no match for home. When she tells him of her plan to return home, she ends with "I have to."[8]

Mom never mentions homesickness when she talks of her early years in America. Maybe time passed differently back then, before WhatsApp and Facebook. When the only real way of communicating was in handwritten letters and Western Union money transfers. Maybe Mom had back then what I see in her now: near-permanent forward-facing-ness. She does not worry over mistakes, she corrects them. She does not dwell on hurt, she squeezes through it.

To her, we are all meant to be stained by the blood of the Lamb, salvation the great equalizer that erases distinction, that dissolves the color line. But when a thing is bled of color, when every tint and hue and cast is washed away, chemistry tells us there can only be white.

So I imagine her in chapel, having cleared her church pew, neither flummoxed by the white people who refuse to sit next to her, nor caught in longing for a place where people who looked like her were the norm and not the exception, not aching with longing for home, but simply adaptive. That first instance, though, must have shocked her, how something so white could be so cold.

Great Expectations

Ifemelu's initial arrival in America carries that quint-essential aspect of the immigrant experience: the swift breaking-down of illusions. Few people are skinny, the streets look nothing like they do in *The Cosby Show*, and the country and its pathologies weigh down on those loved ones who arrived before her. In true immigrant fashion, Ifemelu stays with relatives, namely her Aunty Uju, who, back in Nigeria, had been partnered with a military officer who lavished her with gifts and seemed to provoke in Uju a sophisticated manner, crafted in opposition to the man's own crude disposition. But Aunty Uju wasn't just rich; she had been wealthy. Wealth—true wealth—injects into its owner an air not just of confidence but of dominion. Rich means having coin to spend. Wealth means retaining the rights to the very land you walk on. And yet Uju is "subdued"[9] by America. She works three jobs and, having already been a medical professional in Nigeria, must retrain in a system that validates test-taking over actual knowledge. She is not only back at Square One, she is a Black immigrant, which casts her even deeper into a negative space.

Ifemelu befriends a Grenadian couple: Marlon and Jane, who have two children, Elizabeth and Junior. A point of connection between Ifemelu and Jane: the similarities of their childhoods in their respective countries. "Enid Blyton books and Anglophile teachers and fathers who worshipped the BBC World Service."[10]

Adichie writes:

> They would sit together on the front steps of the building and watch Dike and Jane's children, Elizabeth and Junior, ride their bicycles to the end of the street and then back, Ifemelu often calling out to Dike not to go any farther, the children shouting, the concrete sidewalks gleaming in the hot sun,

and the summer lull disrupted by the occasional rise and fall of loud music from passing cars.[11]

The Brooklyn neighborhood that serves as the initial landing pad for Aunty Uju and her son, Dike, is coated in a type of meteorological kindness. I recognized this from my own youth. One afternoon in particular, at our home in post-industrial New Britain, Connecticut, a summer thunderstorm caught us outside. A bunch of us, me and my sister and a friend of hers and my brother, ran up and down our street as the sky turned blood-red and raindrops as fat as balloons splashed on our faces, raindrops so big you could dodge them.

During that summer thunderstorm, the air was so warm and the raindrops so bulbous, that the impulse to seek shelter and dry out escaped us completely, even as thunder boomed perilously soon after the lightning. We bathed in that storm. We roared with laughter.

While we were doing this, my mother was cleaning office spaces throughout Connecticut, with my father taking out their trash and vacuuming their floors and cleaning their toilets, having already completed her Master's degree.

Suddenly, my mother was Uju, and I became Dike.

* * *

Americanah reminded me of another way in which the experience of African immigrants subverts their own expectations: the perspective of immigrants towards African Americans. In Nigeria, African-American is a thing to aspire to. It is a way of walking, of talking. It's a certain shade of skin tone, a cultured disposition. In America, however, it is a thing to be spurned and avoided.

Jane sends Elizabeth to a private school, because "'the public schools here are useless. Marlon says we'll move to the suburbs soon so they can go to better schools. Otherwise she will start behaving like these black Americans.'"[12]

Later in the book, Ifemelu takes a job as a nanny to a wealthy white family filled with Americans who fancy themselves liberals. They hold galas to raise money for African children skinny with starvation. Kimberly is the woman who hires her while her sister, Laura, displays a tactless, aggressive affection for Ifemelu, "researching" Nigerians and asking Ifemelu about 419 scams and remittance practices.

One day, Laura returns from the doctor's office with a story:

> I took [Athena] to her follow-up from the ear infection and she's been an absolute bear all day.

Oh and I met the most charming Nigerian man
today. We get there and it turns out a new doctor
has just joined the practice and he's Nigerian and
he came by and said hello to us. He reminded me
of you, Ifemelu. I read on the Internet that Nigerians are the most educated immigrant group in
this country. Of course, it says nothing about the
millions who live on less than a dollar back in your
country, but when I met the doctor I thought of
that article and of you and other privileged Africans who are in this country.[13]

Shocked at being called "privileged," Ifemelu thinks
of a man named Kayode DeSilva, "whose passport
sagged with the weight of visa stamps, who went to
London for summer and to Ikoyi Club to swim, who
could casually get up and say 'We're going to Frenchies
for ice cream.'"[14]

Dissatisfied with Dr. Bingham, Laura determines to
switch Athena's doctor to this new Nigerian man. She
then mentions a woman she once met in graduate school
from Uganda. "'She was wonderful, and she didn't get
along with the African-American woman in our class.
She didn't have all those issues.'"[15]

When the white family entertains guests, a man calls Ifemelu beautiful by comparing her to Ethiopian women. Beneath the compliment is the suggestion that Ifemelu is this way because she is not like American Blacks.

For Our Own Good

Throughout my childhood and adolescence, Mom seemed to stress that our "difference" in this country stemmed not from us being Black but from us being a family of immigrants. Even then, I detected in her tone the admonition that we were not supposed to behave "like them." Aunty Uju uproots Dike and moves to Massachusetts, not only to be with her new boyfriend, another Nigerian man named Bartholomew, but because she believes Dike has begun misbehaving. "'Where did he learn that from?'"[16] Aunty Uju laments, blaming those "wild children with no home training"[17] at his daycare. And I often wonder where Mom learned to make that distinction. Though the picture I've painted of Liberty University so far has been that of a bastion of staunch conservatism, the soil cultivating the Moral Majority, I am sure that there were liberal whites there, or at least whites who, like Kimberly and Laura, fancied themselves liberal. Righteous whites, but whose righteousness was not relevant.

I wonder if Mom saw her separateness, and ours, as part of a hierarchy. Those compliments about her English and about her poise and about her intelligence bring to mind those well-meaning but ultimately back-handed compliments Frantz Fanon must have received from whites during his time in Lyon, the presence of these quintessentially "white" qualities evidence that he was not like "them"—this time Africans and, specifi-cally, Algerians. Cleverness, articulation—these were not "Black" traits.

I'd been raised in predominantly white neighbor-hoods, had attended predominantly white schools, and had found myself among predominantly white church members. I wonder if Mom saw in the lives of her chil-dren an opportunity to keep them safe, away from the plight of Blackness.

Was Blackness a trap? Quicksand?

Maybe Mom saw what American Blacks endured in this country, saw the symptoms without recognizing the sickness, and, in ultimate maternal fashion, sought to keep us safe and warm in the myth of meritocracy.

To be Black in America was to be hated, by others and by self. Who could blame her for wanting to chart for her children a different destiny?

PART 2

THE OTHER SIDE OF SUFFERING

American Black

Two characters in *Americanah* prompt Ifemelu's growing political awareness of American Blackness: her true love Obinze and her second serious American boyfriend Blaine. Her learning, in both instances, arises out of love. In both cases, a desire to know another person plunges Ifemelu into the works of American writers and the workings of American politics.

In Chapter 14, as Ifemelu begins her collegiate career, Obinze encourages her to begin reading the works of James Baldwin. Until then, so much of America is contradiction and mystery. But then "[I]n his first e-mail to her—a cyber-cafe had just opened in Nsukka—he gave her a list of books. *The Fire Next Time* was first."[1]

Adichie writes of Ifemelu:

She stood by the library shelf and skimmed the opening chapter, braced for boredom, but slowly she moved to a couch and sat down and kept reading until three-quarters of the book was gone, then she stopped and took down every James Baldwin title on the shelf. [...] She wrote to Obinze about the books she read, careful, sumptuous letters that opened, between them, a new intimacy; she had begun, finally, to grasp the power books had over him. His longing for Ibadan because of "Ibadan" had puzzled her; how could a string of words make a person ache for a place he did not know? But in those weeks when she discovered the rows and rows of books with their leathery smell and their promise of pleasures unknown, when she sat, knees tucked underneath her on an armchair in the lower level or at a table upstairs with the fluorescent light reflecting off the book's pages, she finally understood. [...] And as she read, America's mythologies began to take on meaning, America's tribalisms— race, ideology, and region—became clear. And she was consoled by her new knowledge.[2]

A brief memory, prompted by a classroom episode, follows on the next few pages:

> Ifemelu had first watched *Roots* on video with Obinze and his mother, sunk into sofas in their living room in Nsukka. As Kunta Kinte was being flogged into accepting his slave name, Obinze's mother got up abruptly, so abruptly she almost tripped on a leather pouf, and left the room, but not before Ifemelu saw her reddened eyes. It startled her, that Obinze's mother, fully hemmed into her self-containment, her intense privacy, could cry watching a film. Now, as the window blinds were raised and the classroom once again plunged into light, Ifemelu remembered that Saturday afternoon, and how she had felt lacking, watching Obinze's mother, and wishing that she, too, could cry.[3]

In less than a paragraph, Adichie describes the entirety of my high school experience. Not only is the tragedy of the African-American plight a removed thing, examined from a distance, clinically, but I see how depictions and discussions of it impact those around me, and I find myself wishing I could react as they did. For the first time in my life, seeing my high school classmates, I wanted it. I wanted their hurt, their anguish. I wanted the outrage, and I wanted it to feel genuine coming from me. "Injustice anywhere is a threat to justice everywhere,"[4] writes Dr. Martin Luther King in his "Letter from a Birmingham Jail." The quote always struck true, but again there was that remove. No one in my family had endured the 1963 Birmingham Race Riots. No pressurized firehoses had been aimed our way. None of us had been whipped into servility, our families separated, our entire existence reduced to function and measures of productivity. No one had redlined us, and, even then, I had no recollection of ever having been called a nigger. I understood less that the word hurt than that it was meant to hurt.

That particular distinction drives the ensuing class discussion, and I must note with a bit of hilarity the horror on Professor Moore's face as a Kenyan student, Wambui, and an African-American student battle it out over whether or not the word *nigger* should have been bleeped out of the recording of *Roots* they have just finished watching.

It makes no sense to Wambui, who is characterized throughout the scene as having "a firm voice."[5] It is evidence of denial. Ifemelu, having recently read

William Faulkner's *Light in August*, takes a logic-based approach, positing that the word can be judged based on the (color of the) speaker. When the African-American student asserts that the word shouldn't be used at all because of its elementally injurious nature—it has no other purpose than to wound—and because no matter whose mouth it comes from, murderous intent powers its voicing, the Kenyan student replies, "'If my mother hits me with a stick and a stranger hits me with a stick, it's not the same thing.'"[6]

The white students are wisely silent as the debate plays out, and one finds in the professor a sense that the ship she has so confidently steered, indeed with a sort of lackadaisical insouciance, has ventured into choppy waters, frustrating her efforts to control it. Is there any way for a white professor to adroitly and constructively guide a discussion on the meaning and the meaning of usage of the "n-word"? You attempt at your own peril.

But what did it say that the only way I could imagine myself into an identity as an African American was along the third rail of historical hurt? It seemed that the most salient difference between American Blacks and me was that horrible things had happened to them. Horrible things specific to the history of the American polity and woven into the very fabric of its being, blood poisoning specific soil in specific fashion.

For me, until high school, "American Black" was a collection of stereotypes and a haphazard assemblage of lived experiences. That changed during the spring of my senior year when I took my first academic course on Blackness, a class with a Reverend on "the Black Experience." Every week, we were to write reaction papers to the previous week's readings: essays by abolitionist and women's rights activist Maria Stewart, abolitionist David Walker, historian and activist Vincent Harding. It is the first time I remember referring to American Blacks as "my people." Reading Stewart, I was finally forced to face the notion of morality as a form of rescue, not merely deprivation. To be moral was to rescue yourself from hatred. Grow an intellect, nurse your talents, and thus be convinced of your own nobility.

She writes:

> Would not our brethren fall in love with their virtues? Their souls would become fired with a holy zeal for freedom's cause. They would become ambitious to distinguish themselves; they would become proud to display their talents. Able advocates would arise in our defense. Knowledge would

begin to flow, and the chains of slavery and ignorance would melt like wax before the flames....[7]

After I read David Walker, I saw Stewart's entreaties as dripping with docility and servitude.

Walker's words breathed fire into my lungs:

They (the whites) know well, if we are men—and there is a secret monitor in their hearts which tells them we are—they know, I say, if we are men, and see them treating us in the manner they do, that there can be nothing in our hearts but death alone, for them, notwithstanding we may appear cheerful, when we see them murdering our dear mothers and wives, because we cannot help ourselves. Man, in all ages and all nations of the earth, is the same.[8]

In an essay on Jim Crow, I wrote:

Men often fear what is different, what they cannot understand, what is, in some cases, beyond them. With this fear can come anger, hate, injustice. Men wish to eliminate the difference, to suppress the fact that there exists something they cannot comprehend. They wish to control it. This can be said of Jim Crow in relation to the Black experience. In

the civil rights movement, it can be said that for
every step forward, there have been two steps back-
ward. For every changed amendment, hundreds
of African Americans were killed or lynched. For
every bill or law passed granting further freedoms
to blacks, a family was slaughtered.

That opening line came not from any inchoate
understanding of race relations in America or from any
real lived experience. It was a mantra I had heard several
times while watching *X-Men: The Animated Series*.

Re-reading this and other response papers, it is easy
to see the almost antiseptic quality of the writing, shot
through on occasions with bits of opprobrium and
outrage, but sterile nonetheless.

In that same essay:

Fear was another predominant element in the
whole Jim Crow mentality. If the Negroes won't
submit when we ask nicely, then we'll coerce
them into it, we'll beat them into it. We'll make
them too scared to do otherwise. That was the
mentality of the white majority during Jim Crow.
Joseph Holloway recounts how in Waco, Texas,
he witnessed a black man on fire and screaming
and still very alive. In his testimony, he talks

about the 500 men, women, and children that nearly made him the victim of another lynching. In Wilmington, North Carolina—an oasis of racial harmony—fear drove its citizens and their neighbors in an uproarious frenzy, exterminating or totally removing the black population from that town. Black men were removed from office, houses torched, families shot, men lynched. All out of fear. It is an inherent primitive reaction to a phenomenon, and it is not the blacks who are reduced to portrayal as animals; it is the whites! They were no different from the bloodthirsty Romans who cried and cheered and pumped their fists in the air as lions devoured helpless Christians! They, who wore their Sunday dress to attend a public lynching! They, who laughed and mocked as the blackened corpse writhed and danced in its noose! They, whose ears held both the cries of the black man and the words of the minister delivered hours before! It is the greatest irony that the truest animals thought themselves better than the blacks they shared a country with.

As adept as I've become at time-travel, I cannot voyage deep enough into my teenage mind to tell where those exclamation points came from. Whether they were borne of personal hurt and a sense that I, in some way, shape, or form, was being targeted by race hatred; whether they were meant to highlight the absurdity of the picture—whites who fancy themselves upstanding donning their Sunday best to attend the gruesome mutilation and murder of another human being—or whether those exclamation points were a mask I felt it appropriate to wear, I can't tell. Doubt niggles at the back of my mind; the people-pleaser in me that allowed me to so gracefully work a room and that had made me such an adroit conversation partner was here at work as well, hunting for a good grade.

Until that point, the world had been exceedingly kind to me. Cloistered in that boarding school with every resource at my disposal and lacking for absolutely nothing, American Blackness was history. What reason did I have to believe that any of what had happened to *them* would someday happen—was already happening—to *me*?

But something had stirred in me, learning about America's history of terrorizing Black people. It was wrong. And it angered me.

What vocabulary I had for articulating that anger, I owe to the Palestinians.

Intifada

My political education began the spring prior, in 2004, when I was introduced to the Palestinians.

I was a junior in high school and had elected to take a course on the Contemporary Middle East. The beginning of that semester marked the one-year anniversary of the US invasion of Iraq. Our teacher forced us to read the *New York Times* and the *Wall Street Journal* every morning, copies of which were left at our dining hall tables during breakfast. The Second Intifada, bloodier and more pitched than the First, having shrugged off the stole of civil disobedience, was one year from its official end. Every morning, I dutifully scanned those central columns in the *Wall Street Journal*, noting which Hamas or Islamic Jihad leader had been killed in a targeted strike the day before.

Blood stained the floors of cafés in Haifa, blanketed the carpeting of hotel lobbies in Tel Aviv. Katyusha rockets became their own form of precipitation. Which was why I would leave class, week after week, confused as to why I felt the way I did for the Palestinian Arabs, why I felt the chief injustice was the one happening to them.

As had been demonstrated by the material, this was a complicated region, steeped in history. I was told that if you held a single stone to your ear, you would hear it shout at you in both Hebrew and Arabic. Maybe I had missed something. Maybe the Palestinian Arabs were asking for more than I thought they were asking for.

Maybe so, too, were African Americans.

* * *

What I carried from high school into college was the notion that identity was a sort of diamond, the coal of multilayered geographical vectors pressurized by suffering into a coruscating core of self. Suffering was the philosopher's stone that transmuted the self into the nation.

In my sophomore year of college, I wrote a research paper on the development of Palestinian nationalism in the West Bank and the East during the period of Jordan's annexation of the West—until then, my most titanic academic endeavor. In an introductory section, I identify Palestinian identity as "a set of overlapping identities, not so much layers as threads in a tapestry. It was not uncommon to come across a man who identified as a Muslim, an Arab, a Nablusi, a South Syrian and an Ottoman. Identity in that region carried ethnic, religious, familial, and transnational dimensions, each of which was based on an affiliation that coexisted with the others." Waves of Jewish immigration (the first *Aliya* from 1882-1903 and the second from 1903-1914), in my jejune analysis, nudge Palestinian identity not into any sort of nationalism as popularly understood but into a deeper land-based ipseity. What autonomous political community could Palestinian Arabs lay emotive claim to?

Nineteen forty-eight provided the cataclysm that catalyzes what many would look at in the decades to follow as Palestinian nationalism. Whether rich or poor, literate or illiterate, urban or rural, the Palestinians endured this Nakba as a whole. Displacement gave them a shared political fate. It is war, according to Palestinian American historian Rashid Khalidi, that serves as the "great leveller, and a source of universally shared experience".[9]

So, whether they were from Nablus or Jerusalem or Hebron or Gaza City and whether they ended up in Sidon, Khan Younis, Neirab, or Souf, they were Palestinians.

Julie Peteet, in her 2005 book *Landscape of Hope and Despair: Palestinian Refugee Camps*, writes:

> For Palestinians, the camps embodied multiple, sometimes contradictory and ambiguous meanings. Social location is crucial in discussing these

representations and imaginings. For their residents, they were places of sanctuary as well as zones of cultural celebration in a hostile world. To Palestinians on the exterior, they epitomized cultural purity, suffering, and resistance. Because they housed the resistance and refugees who had previously been peasants, they were places of an authentic Palestinian identity rooted in the land, struggle, and suffering.[10]

The context for the excerpt is the 1970s. And the place: Palestinian refugee camps in Lebanon.

It is clear at this point that the refugee camps in Egypt, Jordan, Syria, and Lebanon are no longer temporary solutions to the problem of displacement but rather semi-permanent features of these host countries. Within them boils the premier Palestinian impetus of repatriation. Around this goal, diasporic communities congregate. And arm themselves.

Identification spreads even further, lending Palestinian identity a marked elasticity.

So strong was the emphasis on the struggle for repatriation that the term "Palestinian" began to transcend its former dimensions, including, for the first time, foreigners and those very clearly not of Middle Eastern descent. In this era of training camps blossoming over the globe, Russian mercenaries could be considered just as Palestinian as a Galilean-born Arab. Commitment to the struggle was the salient dimension of identity. The plan launched by the Hashemite Kingdom of Jordan to integrate the Palestinian population of the West Bank was failing.

That paper on Palestinian nationalism introduced me to a term I would return to in a later class on post-colonial political thought. It provided a solution to my earlier quandary. Because, as I would soon discover, the other side of suffering is self-determination.

* * *

I used to wonder what it was that drew me so early on—as early as high school—to the plight of the Palestinians. Initial answers were that the conflict that seemed to define them as a people took place in a land to which my religious upbringing made constant refer-ences. Bethlehem was a real place; so was Jerusalem. Hebron, Galilee, Nazareth. All sites of Biblical signifi-cance, all tangible realities with dirt and buildings and living, breathing, ever-present people in them.

But I think a greater draw was the violence. Before I knew what the Palestine-Israel conflict was, I knew there were guns in it. I had started reading John Le Carré novels in high school, and spy novels fought to replace speculative fiction as my amour fou. I found my international itch scratched. Bullets and bombs made ideas terrifyingly terrestrial.

As with so many things in my life, what began as an academic fascination blossomed swiftly into a personal fixture. Palestine opened a door for me onto the wider world of postcolonialism. It introduced me to refugees and liberation struggles. It introduced me to Frantz Fanon, and yet another thread in the braid of Blackness.

Wretched

If self-determination is the engine of the nation-state, then its microcosmic analog is self-actualization. And while Fanon's most popular bequest is the blueprint and bible for decolonization, *The Wretched of the Earth*, I first met him in *Black Skin, White Masks*. In the book sits Fanon, the radical humanist bent on breathing new life into the golems that had been made of the colonized, fashioning new, self-actualized men, who, farther down the line in his literary project, would go about the business of nation-building. Fanon as psychiatrist. Physician, heal thyself.

In some sense, *Black Skin, White Masks* could be read as a dissertation.[11] Indeed, its original title was *Essay on the Disalienation of the Black*. It can read as addressed to its subject, or it can be read by a disinterested third party as a socio-historical treatise on psychic rupture suffered by French Caribbean peoples torn between emotive fealty to a distant metropole and the urge to rebel against it. In the way that speculative fiction can operate as reality and metaphor simultaneously, so did racism and the racist gaze for Fanon. The colonizer's treatment of the colonized[12] (both passive and active), rendering the Black person an object and caging the possibilities of their lived experience within the confines of a skin-color construction, does to the colonized what neurological disease does to the dyad of soma and psyche.

> Beneath the body schema I had created a historical-racial schema. The data I used were not provided by remnants of feeling and notions of the tactile, vestibular, kinesthetic, or visual nature but by the Other, the white man, who had woven me out of a thousand details, anecdotes, and stories.[13]

Even at the end of his quadrilogy—*The Wretched of the Earth* and its sanguine pathos having unseated the earlier repudiation of eye-for-an-eye in *Black Skin, White Masks*—Fanon the physician is there. By now, however, we have moved from the quasi-metropole of Fort de France to the bombed-out byways of Algiers. Toward the end of *Wretched*, Fanon details[14] in almost clinical fashion the psychological tax exacted from both sides in the Algerian War for Independence:

1. Impotence in an Algerian following the rape of his wife
2. Undifferentiated homicidal impulses found in a survivor of a mass murder
3. Marked anxiety psychosis of the depersonalization type after the murder of a woman while temporarily insane
4. A European policeman in a depressed state meets while under hospital treatment one of his victims, an Algerian patriot who is suffering from stupor
5. A European police inspector who tortured his wife and children
6. The murder by two young Algerians [...] of their European playmate
7. Accusatory delirium and suicidal conduct disguised as "terrorist activity" in a young Algerian twenty-two years old

8. Neurotic attitude of a young Frenchwoman whose father, a highly placed civil servant, was killed in an ambush

9. Behavior disturbances in young Algerians under age ten

Fanon meant his words not only for the marksman, but for the mathematician as well.

But Fanon was writing as an intermediary of sorts. Early in *Toward the African Revolution*, Fanon points at the absurdity of the blanket term "Negro people"[15] as it assumes that all people of a certain gradient of melanin constitute a behavioral monolith. He points out that in lumping the West Indian and the African together like that, one would be committing the same sort of folly as lumping together a "Brazilian and a Spaniard".[16] The logical fallacy is obvious: at work in the two regions of the West Indies and North Africa are different socio-cultural dynamics, as well as different economic battlegrounds on which daily encounters along the social stratum play out, to say nothing of Africa as an infinitely complex polity and landscape on its own. But then Fanon goes on to point out the superiority of the West Indian to the African, pontificating as though the quality were something inherent rather than part of the colonial construct foisted upon them by their civil administrators. "The West Indian was not a Negro; he was a West Indian, that is to say quasi-metropolitan," writes Fanon. "By this attitude the white man justified the West Indian in his contempt for the African."[17]

Granted, Fanon's tone is slightly facetious and serves to highlight the ignominy of the attitudes of the colonial administration. But it aptly tracks the changing dynamic between two sectors of the "Negro people" before and after the wartime shocks that ruptured the collective worldview of Martinicians—namely Martinician poet and politician Aimé Césaire's public affirmation of the glory of his dark skin, France's military losses, and the role of domestic traitors in that failure. The white light is no longer the end goal, and new comfort is found in claiming identity as a Negro. Thus, in both practice and attitude, the West Indian "returns" to Africa to a variety of responses from Africans. What is essentially at play is a difference in colonial situations, even though both the West Indies and much of Northern Africa are prey to the particular demon of French colonialism. In Algeria, "French colonialism is a war force; it has to be beaten down by force."[18] But for Martinicians, it seems something much more bloodless. Still, as a crisis of identity, it is just as existential.

In the dehistoricized narratives that follow the death of anti-colonialist thinkers like Fanon, at least when the story of the savannah is told by the hunter, the firebrand is typically reduced to a slogan or a sterile academic study. Or, in the case of Dr. Martin Luther King Jr., a colorless New Testament collection of appeals to lazy harmony. This suggests that the historical figure began as an angry, misguided visionary before being made wise by pacifism.

Fanon was never a pacifist. He believed in the utility of violence.

It is all one process to Fanon. The individual must first self-actualize and consider himself intrinsically equal to his oppressor before he can begin contemplating the task of national liberation, which is a collective effort made by a cabal of self-actualized individuals. Violence is the thread that holds it together. It begins by combating the psychological violence brought on by systemic domination dynamics, then combating the physical violence by overthrowing the tangible and institutional manifestations of that dominance dynamic. That is the liberation project. That is how both the individual and the nation can realize their own importance.

* * *

Between midnight and 2:00 a.m. on November 1, 1954, the Front de Libération Nationale (FLN) carried out a series of 30 bomb attacks and acts of sabotage against police and military installations throughout French Algeria, killing seven, all of whom except two were French colonists. Five Pied-Noir civilians, two Algerians. *Toussaint Sanglante* marked the beginning of a war that would last seven years, four months, two weeks, and four days. It would lead to the demise of the Fourth French Republic, a mass exodus of some 900,000 Pieds-Noirs, and, with its militarization of politics and its valorization of external jihad, it would lay out a design for both leftwing revolutionaries and Islamic fundamentalists. In collectively appropriating violence, the colonized have actualized their agency.

Fanon arranged for FLN meetings to be held at the hospital in Bilda where he worked, treating the wounds of FLN fighters while barring entry to French soldiers who refused to lay down their arms, and instructing FLN fighters on how to control their body language to best mask their intentions to throw grenades or plant bombs. How to disguise themselves, essentially, from the police.

Throughout, Fanon proposed a nationalism made of will rather than simply birthright. Algerian nationalism was an *esprit de corps*, Algerian identity a thing to be earned. He would never be French; French whites would never allow such psychological assimilation, despite the primacy his being a Martinician bestowed on him over the African, not a mimeo of Europe but a mimicry. "Look, maman, a Negro!"[19] So, he transfers his fierce identification with a country that had spurned him to its opposite in the Manichean dialogue. Algerian identity, in his eyes, stretches even beyond the borders of birthplace and ethnicity, and becomes rooted in the simple desire for justice, however violent it may prove. You cannot be Algerian if you do not burn with rage for the injustices perpetrated by whites in the Rhodesias and in Angola.

Hebron

The summer of 2013, between my first and second years of law school, I lived in the West Bank, working for a prisoners' rights organization that advocated for the release of Palestinian Arab detainees held in Israeli prisons under the policy of administrative detention. I was part of a group of Americans sent to various organizations that had various specializations: land rights, women's rights, etc.

One afternoon, our group went to Hebron.

We passed west around Bethlehem, a long road with Biblical landscape on both sides, tiered green hills, moss and grass spread over stone. Settlements dotted the fields, trailers on both sides of the shared road that presaged larger homes and the eventual colonization of that road after Government Forces connected the services, electricity and water, of the two small communities.

Downtown Hebron looked very much like many other downtowns I'd seen in urban Palestine: older men crowded at a Bank of Jordan ATM, adolescents in t-shirts and jeans congregating outside a mall, hijabi women and young men in stylish button-downs. On this part of Shuhada Street, there were no Israelis. But as we walked further, a trailer came into view, blocking the street. In it was a metal detector and a few Israeli soldiers. On a balcony overhead, an olive-uniformed soldier, assault rifle draped across his body, waved at us, mocking.

In Hebron, roads to homes are cut off and many Palestinians have to negotiate through the houses of their neighbors or over rooftops to return from work in the evenings.

Eyes on the trailer, we listened to our guide tell us of the February '94 massacre when a Jewish settler, a doctor, entered the Ibrahimi Mosque, the city's holiest site, and opened fire on the men and women praying within, killing 29 and wounding over 100. He told us of how the military and the settlers occupied wholesale markets, cutting off fruit supply, how one day a group of settlers rented rooms at a local Arab hotel and refused to leave, departing only after they had turned the building over to the Yesha, the local Settlement Council, a trade our guide likened to individual gangsters handing their conquest over to mob bosses. The settlers and the settlement associations deal with each other, not the Palestinians they steal from, said our guide with no small amount of acid.

The city is divided into two sectors: H-1, governed by the Palestinian Authority; and H-2, governed by Israel. The borders are often marked by red signs warning away the other side, and you can see, passing through these gateways, dead areas where shops have closed down.

A group of teens walked by, one of them angrily kicking a soda can, on their way to the border trailer.

We passed through the trailer and on the other side of the checkpoint was a patch of ghost town. Occasional police vehicles with Hebrew on their fronts and their flanks lounged on street corners. The roads were paved by American funds, the shuttered storefronts doused in uniform American-supplied paint, the windows overhead barred by metal grating to protect the remaining Arab residents on this side of the division from the stones thrown by the settlers on the street. When the muezzin chants over the empty street, one feels haunted.

At the corner of Beit Hadassa, at the end of the street, Palestinians turn right, go around through the Muslim cemetery, then come back down another hill to arrive at the southern part of the city, instead of taking the path straight ahead.

Often, in between trailers, there are no signs demarcating these boundaries; one simply knows where one can walk and where one can't.

In the market, back in the Palestinian section of town, there are tables laden with sunglasses, hats, food, jeans, dresses, shirts, backpacks, almonds, scarves, flats, heels, teapots, cosmetics. And behind a fence are the settlers whose garden we peeked into earlier. There's a dead end by the fence, and while we walked through the market, store owners and hawkers peppered us with *Where-are-you-from*s.

If you crane your neck and look up, you'll notice a grate overhead, heavy with metal bars and bricks and bottles, socks filled with feces and urine and occasional residue from acid thrown earlier. Detritus.

Things the Jewish settlers have aimed at the Palestinian market below.

There's a bridge overhead, several meters down, that the settlers use for a new angle of attack sometimes.

Further down, children in sweats and tanktops and soccer shirts kick around a half-deflated soccer ball, knock it against shuttered storefronts, horseplay. Then there's a section of the souk that's been abandoned.

Past that, one can see, through the barbed-wire fence, a Yeshiva school, guarded by Israeli soldiers in various towers bedecked with security cameras. This school was built on top of a Palestinian school that the Arab children, for obvious reasons, have stopped attending.

Further down the street, past a building scarred by a long, vertical fracture, is a stone plaque in Hebrew, commemorating the first settler murdered in Hebron. Stabbed. Palestinians will occasionally come by and paint over the plaque, and settlers will arrive later (sometimes during the Saturday settler tours) and clean it.

You see, in the eyes of the younger people, a quiet coiled violence; in the posture of the women the silent strength born of furious continuance; while the older men are buried beneath their eyebrows, their frowns hidden under the shade cast by their mustaches.

Construction often indicates settler homes built on top of Palestinian dwellings. And on the ground through this main market street is stomped shit from animals that are nowhere to be seen. A cross street to the wholesale market is blocked by a metal panel, and when it rains, it all drains down this street, ruining the markets and the buildings.

Adolescents in the darkened hallway shout at each other louder than necessary. I saw an older brother, a storefront manager, corralling them with a long stick, eventually smacking one of the kids who ran, screaming, weeping, past us.

What's the difference between an Arab and a diving board, our guide asked us. You step on a diving board without shoes, was the answer.

Near a jewelry shop was a board showing instances of settler violence and the homes the settlers build, their own fellowship with each other juxtaposed against the violence they used to build this place. Where we stood then, the Abraham Avril settlement looked down on us.

The cobblestone street outside of a café further down was soaked in effulgence. Opposite us, children banged on a metal door, and I didn't know if they meant to open it further or close it.

At the very end of the street was a turnstile, a security checkpoint. To the immediate left after that was another security detail just outside the Ibrahimi Mosque, which is said to be the burial site of Abraham two thousand years ago on land purchased from Arabs.

Inside the mosque, the floor is laden with red-patterned carpets, a few fans spinning lazily, shoeless men reclining against the walls. The women in our group were given blue and brown hooded shawls, covering their hair and their arms. This was one of the rooms where the massacre occurred. Throughout the space are monuments marking the tombs of martyrs buried in a cave beneath our feet. Koranic scripture can be seen along the upper area of the walls, draping the columns, fans periodically hanging over their strips. Our guide tells us of a time when the Jews and the Muslims would worship here together. The building itself is segregated. The mosque area is opened to Muslims and tourists who are not Jewish, the synagogue opened to Israeli Jews, Christians, and tourists who aren't Muslim. At the gate, a security officer asks your religion. Our tour guide told the officer we were all Christians. Along the enclave and the colonnade surrounding it, the bullet holes from the massacre are marked by small bits of paper that say 'S24' and 'S43,' other impacts similarly marked. An attachment to the mosque looks out onto the Abraham monument, and past that, the Sarah monument. Isaac, Jacob, and Joseph of the many-colored coat are also said to have been at one point interred here. It seemed profane to take pictures in there. On the other side of a wall, Russian Jews chanted, shouting over our tour guide's voice. They seemed only to hear themselves. In the shoe storage area, there's Arabic script above Sarah's tomb praising the city's last Turkish settlers from long ago, and above that, an Israeli security camera. When the mosque is crowded, the men and women worship separately. When it isn't, they worship in the same room.

On a hill next to the mosque entrance is a gate with armed Israeli guards barring access to another Israeli/Jewish area of town. Five Palestinian families remain there and must pass through two checkpoints, one at the top of the hill and one at the bottom, to leave their street. They are forbidden from inviting friends over for tea. Once those families are convinced to move out, settlers will take their place.

Down by a barricade segregating the Arab and Jewish parts of town, a kid huckster charmed us in French. We passed through the barricade to arrive at a blockaded street blanketed in quiet but thick with tension, like when a Black man walks into an all-white bar. Israeli soldiers with M16s guarded the barricade, olive green uniforms, banana clips held together by black tape. As we leave, other soldiers erect a new barrier at the other end of the street.

On our way back through a previous checkpoint, a soldier manning the booth has his rifle aimed lethargically at the opposite entrance.

We turned a corner and passed through a tunnel that opened out onto a playground and adjacent plaza. Kids in open air. I finally found the goats, who were corralled in a separate pen. Children in a row by the swings chased us along, one of them giving marching orders in Arabic with a stick he had found.

Hebron in 2013 made me wonder what Belfast in 1993 must have looked like. Or Birmingham in 1963.

If you took Northern Ireland during the Troubles, Jim Crow America, and interwar Germany, and mixed those colors on your palette, you might be able to paint an image resembling Hebron that summer.

There aren't enough tears in my body to weep for the world, and there's not enough rage in the heart to hate all oppressors equally, but I worried about what that place was doing to me. My mother, in response to an email I'd sent her assuring her that I was yet alive, told me not to get consumed by what I saw over there. If my presence there could bring blessing to one person's life, she assured me, then I will have done my duty in the eyes of the Lord. This same woman has exemplified the notion that it's not enough to beat the Devil once. You have to wake up and knock him down every single day. I thought that was only true of inner battles, but I saw it there too. Jewish Israelis aren't the Devil, nor is Israel the embodiment of evil. But it is difficult, titanically so, to leave a place like Hebron without hate in your heart.

* * *

The pain will pass. When running against the wind, be sure to keep calm. Don't touch your face. Do not rinse with water. Use Coca-Cola or milk instead to end the burning. If you are close enough to the police, they cannot use the tear gas on you. And in the event that you are without a gas mask, you can wrap a t-shirt around your nose and mouth and protect your eyes with goggles or something similar. The oblong tear gas canisters are small enough that they can be hurled back at the shooter before too much gas is expelled. To properly douse them, be sure to arm yourself with a Poland Springs jug half-filled with water, and the canister that lands beside you, toss it inside, stand on the opening and wave away the remaining fumes as the device is extinguished. If there is fire nearby, toss the canister in the fire, and that too will neutralize it.

This was the advice given to protestors in Ferguson, Missouri in the conflagration that followed the August 2014 murder of 18-year-old Michael Brown by Officer Darren Wilson.

It was given to them over Twitter. By Palestinians.

That Line About Rage

Somali-British poet and essayist Momtaza Mehri writes, in her essay about a documentary on popstar M.I.A.:

> In one home video, a teenage M.I.A. reads a copy of Frantz Fanon's *The Wretched of the Earth*. Behind her is a collage of posters. Wu Tang Clan concert flyers. Muhammad Ali. Public Enemy. To M.I.A. and generations of non-black children of immigrants, the black radical tradition and its cultural inheritances serve as a source of identity. The black diaspora is a North Star for racialized youngsters seeking self-discovery. What better way to do so than through the transatlantic swagger of masculinist black power politics? Amid Brit-pop's exaggerated oikiness, it's no coincidence that M.I.A. and many like her were energized by

black expressive culture. After all, who can resist the slick-talking, fist-raising and leather-clad symbolism of black cool? Of course, black people are often the last to benefit materially from black cool. When black thinkers become dehistoricized avatars, entire liberation movements are reduced to stylistic embellishments. But therein lies the cruel joke; blackness is lubriciously supple in the hands of non-black people. When lived by actual black people, it is painfully restrictive.[20]

Everyone wants to be Black until it's time to be Black.

I returned to the States after that summer in Palestine with a newfound fury at the American carceral complex. While I was in the West Bank, many of our clients and their associates had been engaged in a hunger strike, protesting the conditions of their confinement. An ocean away, inmates throughout California's prisons were doing the same. In my second year of law school, I wrote a long research paper on dueling carceral philosophies developed in the United States (one borne of a fierce procedural fidelity, the other of an impetus towards maintaining a racially stratified social order) and their exportation to foreign countries.

There is academic analysis, sure—hypothesis and explanation and evidence presented—but, re-reading it now, abhorrence is easy to find. I felt I was writing it from the inside. This wasn't my high school self opining on Jim Crow. This was me with friends and acquaintances who had done time in jail and prison. This was me after George Zimmerman's acquittal in the murder of Trayvon Martin. This was me turgid with the understanding that I too was meant for the dragnet. I was not separate. I was not immune. I was prey. I had found the Philosopher's Stone.

Whenever I listen to M.I.A., I feel like I have five different passports, four world phones, homies on every single continent with 50 bajillion languages between us, I'm wearing the flyest dashikis under my bomber jacket, rocking the illest dance moves ever, and my lowtop sneakers have touched every bit of contested territory on both sides of the Atlantic.

I also feel Black. Globally so. Eldridge Cleaver skipping bail after a police attack in Oakland, landing in Havana, then being spirited under cover of darkness to refuge in Algiers. Blackness internationalized.

In 1961, a journal article entitled "The Negro in American Culture" was published in *CrossCurrents* Magazine, styled as a sort of roundtable whose participants included James Baldwin, Emile Capouya, Lorraine Hansberry, Nat Hentoff (moderator), Langston Hughes, and Alfred Kazin. The text is a mildly edited transcription of a radio interview broadcast from WBAI-FM in New York.

Hentoff starts things off:

> HENTOFF: To begin the subject, which sounds alarmingly vague, I'd like to start with the end of the book review that James Baldwin wrote for *The New York Times* a couple of years ago. The review was of poems of Langston Hughes, and you concluded by saying that "he is not the first American Negro to find the war between his social and artistic responsibilities all but irreconcilable." To what extent do you find this true in your own writing in terms of the self-consciousness of being a Negro and a writer, the polarity if it exists?

> BALDWIN: Well, the first difficulty is really so simple that it's usually overlooked: to be a Negro in this country and to be relatively conscious, is to be in a rage almost all of the time.[21]

Baldwin's answer continues, journeying into the tension that belies being a writer writing about an oppressed class—your class—and the dueling duties of documentation and social activism. That line of his has often been repeated to me, stripped of its context, emerging sui generis out of the conflagration that is the Negro's situation in America, whether the year is 1961, 1981, or 2021.

Outside of that line, he expresses that it is not uncommon for the Negro writer to feel a pang of guilt at not being on "the firing line, tearing down the slums and doing all these obviously needed things," which he concedes perhaps wryly are things "other people can do better than you."[22]

That line about rage. I wonder if Ifemelu ever saw it.

When I first came across it, well into my law school years, it felt as though a puzzle piece had been fitted into a place, or as though I had figured out an algebraic proof that had, for all of my life, seemed impossible.

Anyone can be angry. Not everyone can be Black. And not everyone can be American Black.

There's more to it than hurt, though. African-American identity is not contingent entirely upon the horrors that whites have enacted on non-whites.

If, as an American African, I cannot share a history with African Americans, then maybe we can share

TOCHI ONYEBUCHI

a future. Brick by brick, constructing our way into a
shared cathedral.

60

PART 3

IS THIS DESIRE?

Sentimental Education

When I was a child, I nursed a crush on my best friend's older sister. She used to babysit us, and it was the only time, up until middle school, that we could sneak a glimpse of MTV. Mom thought it too "worldly," which is to say, too sinful. Angie, my best friend's sister, would sometimes make homemade popcorn for the occasion. What impressed me the most about this person was how good she was at *Sonic the Hedgehog 2*. The game frustrated me to no end, and I seemed to lack both the motor skills and the cunning that attaining all seven Chaos Emeralds demanded of me. One afternoon, I watched Angie get all of them and beat the game. She breezed through each level, navigated all traps and defeated all bosses. It was the only time I ever saw the game's ending. I stared at her in wonder, mesmerized. Her skill made her godlike.

One day when Mom wasn't home, Angie had the television turned to MTV, and the music video for TLC's "Creep" came on, all wind-rushed satin and faux trumpet playing. I saw the video more than I heard the song, and I remember feeling a warmth in me, starting in my chest before radiating into every extremity. Enough of Mom's churchiness had wormed its way into me to cast the whole experience in the colors of sin. Maybe that's what I'm feeling, I remember thinking. The ardor of transgression.

When Ifemelu partners with her first American boyfriend—Kimberly's cousin, Curt—he likes to say of their origin story that it was "love at first laugh."[1] As Ifemelu recalls, Curt had been visiting from Maryland. Taylor, one of the children Ifemelu babysat, ran into the room, wearing a blue cape and underwear and shouting "I am Captain Underpants,"[2] and, in Curt's eyes, "it was the laugh of a woman who, when she laughed, really laughed."[3] In their quiet moments, Curt teases, "'[Y]ou know what I thought? If she laughs like that, I wonder how she does *other things*.'"[4]

I didn't have the words then that I do now, and I look back with a wry smirk, tinged with sorrow for what will happen in the intervening years. When I saw T-Boz and Left Eye and Chilli, I saw adult women, Black, who were in no way related to me, either by blood or through friendship with my parents. They were unconnected, far enough away to feel safe. And somewhere within that whorl of immorality in which I'd enmeshed myself was a single word. A word that explained what those women meant to me. They were beautiful.

* * *

By the time I read *Americanah*, the idea of "Black love" had become so ingrained in my knowledge as to be unremarkable. I knew it too well. I'd seen it in the couplings of so many of my comrades, the satisfied way they glowed in their act of rebellious self-validation. I'd watched men too interested in maintaining patriarchal superstructures talk about Black Kings and Black Queens, how Black love was a way of reaching back past the obliteration of the history of African America into an era of universal and perpetual excellence. I'd listened to Hoteps talk about how lightning and thunder were the products of our ancestors' lovemaking. And at the other end of the continuum, I saw my mother's fatigued hope that I would marry another Nigerian, specifically an Igbo woman. I don't think it was clannishness that made her wish that for me so much as familiarity. She is an Igbo woman who came from Igbo women. She spent many of her quietest and happiest moments in America in the company of Igbo women. Some of her loudest too. This would make me happy, she surmised.

She nurtured this hope, fed it water and sunlight, even as she raised us around white people, in white neighborhoods, white schools, and white churches. The effect, intended or otherwise, was that statistical probability meant I would spend my formative years figuring out what I thought attractive while surrounded by white girls. For reasons I wouldn't untangle until I was older, they were the only ones I could give my heart to.

I read *Americanah* with no small amount of jealousy. Black people loving Black people, desiring Black people, wanting to fuck and to hold and to comfort and kiss Black people, seemed so natural, so effortless. In that book, I'd seen so many analogs of me and people in my life. Bits of my childhood in Dike, Ifemelu and I both awakening politically on school campuses, Mom and Uju mirrored in their occupational struggles. What would this book, pregnant with the experience of Black people, tell me about love?

Was what happens to Ifemelu, her enduring, fundamental love for Obinze, a thing that could happen to me?

First Kiss

My first kiss was in first grade with a Puerto Rican girl named Maria. Her family wasn't from our neighborhood, but we attended Gaffney Elementary together, and, looking back now, what remains brightest in my memory is her skin, the color of drying shoreline. When we thought no one was looking, she would grab my face or I would grab hers (once I learned the ritual) and we would kiss like in the daytime soap operas we watched when we had the day off from school. I hadn't yet figured out how to show affection (a problem that has only been somewhat mitigated with age), but she seemed light-years ahead of me. Worldly in both senses.

I never told Mom about Maria or our kisses, but I'm reminded of Dike and what Aunty Uju dubs his misbehaving. The incident in question is Dike being caught with a girl from daycare. They're hiding in a closet showing each other their private parts when they're caught. Ifemelu chalks it up to curiosity, but Uju sees the Devil at work. While Maria and I never journeyed into that land, I imagine Mom's reaction would have been similar. She had four children to surveil while Uju had only one, so while Mom might not have uprooted us for Massachusetts, she would have given me the thrashing of my life.

For second grade, Mom moved me and my first sister to a different school. A year later, I had my first crush: Rebekah, a girl who I saw on the first day of school several desks from mine (we were aligned in a row) in a dress so white it encouraged angelic comparison. As though she had alighted, in swift and immediate descent from heaven, to our classroom. Soft-spoken and able to best me on our quizzes in nearly every subject, she played tag with me behind our school building. I wrote her a letter to tell her I liked her, and she told her father, a minister, who wrote me a long and involved and well-meaning letter about love and God's will and walking in the Path, a letter whose contents I've long since forgotten. Indeed, I don't know that I ever fully processed what he wrote, so stricken was I at being spurned in so roundabout a way. My last memory of that letter is of rain-soaked paper, the words in blue cursive bleeding into each other, rivulets that turned the damned thing illegible.

Katherine

While Maria was my first kiss, my first steady girlfriend came in high school. I was at a boarding school in Connecticut and had, early on, found a nearby Baptist church with a thriving youth ministry. This brand of doctrinal instruction was kinder than the fire-and-brimstone of my youth. I attended service on Sundays and would involve myself in some outside activities as well. In the process, I ended up as a bit of a bridge between Town and Gown.

We had our first kiss on a bench outside the Wallingford Public Library while we waited for her mother to pick her up, careful to break away and fix ourselves well before her mother arrived. She would visit me in my dorm room, and I would go to town fairs with her. This was sophomore year, going into my junior fall, and it is the first time I can remember feeling that someone else's heart fluttered in rhythm with my own when we saw each other, when we simply thought of each other.

To this day, my time with Katherine remains charmed in my memory. Our first Valentine's Day together, the walks we would go on, the town fair where we first confessed our feelings for each other. It made no difference that I'd partnered with a Townie. She was gorgeous, and gaining her muscled, Catholic father's stamp of approval remains one of my proudest achievements.

In middle school, I was the only Black kid in my year, which meant that I stumbled through puberty surrounded by thirty-two flavors, all of them vanilla.

Every Black woman in my life was either a blood relation or functionally so. Sisters and cousins and aunties
and Mom. By the time I arrived at high school, all I saw
were sisters and cousins. Even when I met girls from
the Bronx and Chicago and other parts of America that
held realities browner than mine, it never occurred to
me to envision a world where our hearts danced in tune.
At lunch, many of them colonized their tables while I
went to eat with white friends from my dorm or the
football team or the school play. On the few occasions
when I did join them, a fog of reference and cross-refer-
ence hung in the air. Their accents, the volume of their
laughter, the way they ribbed each other—at first there
was a flash of wonder at the glory of it all, but then
came the isolation. We had arrived at this campus from
different worlds. On their planet, their voices and their
bodies spoke a different language and spoke it with a
fluency I could never hope to learn.

Sometimes we would happen upon each other at the
Student Activities Center and, if we were free that afternoon, we'd watch *106 & Park* on BET, and Sean Paul's
music videos would come on and the hosts would talk
about the Nas/Jay-Z beef, and slowly it began to come
together. At the student store, I used money from my
stipend to buy Aaliyah's self-titled album and I played it

on my CD player/alarm clock before I went to bed and after I woke up.

At one point, I DJ'd a show for the campus radio station after a teacher showed me his turntables and how to scratch. Before long, I was gifted CDs, both his and new ones that arrived by virtue of my new position. With the quickness that comes with a young person's neuroplasticity, I learned of Dilated Peoples and Ludacris and Master P. Where in middle school I dove headfirst into metal in many of its varieties, high school entailed a different kind of sorting. I was learning hip-hop. I was learning R&B. Tectonic plates shifted, and suddenly the foundation of a vocabulary was laid, like the learning of vowels and consonants and how accents work on a particular word.

Then would come the interschool dances, the closest thing to a bacchanal that kids of color at prep schools had permission to get into. Again, that sorting. The people who seemed to be having the most fun and who seemed most comfortable in their bodies, most in control of the imaginative ways in which they moved, were the Black and brown kids. I should say by now that I was learning how to breakdance. I could toprock, my 6-step was improving, and though full windmills and flares were a bridge too far, I had a pretty good airswipe, and a well-timed head slide into a freeze would make for a reliably impressive finale. It's still a mystery to me how that happened, probably a simple consequence of my having drifted into the interests my friends carried. But it was my ticket into the dance circles. Then came the moves from the music videos we would watch in the SAC—Sean Paul, Beenie Man, Sisqo, Ja Rule— and suddenly I was closer to these girls than I imagined possible. A flash of TLC, but with industrial quantities of lasciviousness.

Paradise lasted only three to four hours, then those schools that had come to visit—Miss Porter's, Hotch- kiss, Andover, Exeter, sometimes Lawrenceville—would hop back on their buses and head back to their respec- tive campuses. Sometimes we would go to them, which perhaps gave us even more license to boldly discover our physicality absent the prying eyes of prefects or teachers who might recognize us.

There was never any illusion of permanence. We would have our nights, and maybe, once in a while, a number would be exchanged, but I didn't get my first cell phone until my junior year of high school.

Plainly, this was lust, not love. We were bodies, and at the end of the night, we went back to being people. Not until much later did I see the color line. Among the kids who looked like me, I saw limbs and hips and ass and legs and chest. When I was with Katherine, I saw a face.

No one told me I was wrong for feeling the way I did.

* * *

In a shotgun blast of fortuity, the day Ifemelu commits to using her Nigerian accent is the day she meets Blaine—the type of coincidence that only a storyteller can engineer, God and her cosmic choreography. But that first meeting fizzles into nothingness, time passes, and in the interval, Ifemelu endures unrequited crushes as well as occasionally baffling relationships, a few of her partners white.

Ifemelu's first serious relationship after her love back home—the true one that operates as the vertebrae of the narrative—is with Curt. She has committed to her most Nigerian self, as much as she can within the confines of this America she is still discovering, and this, like the liatris that draws the bee, attracts a handsome, rich, white man around whom good fortune seems to organize.

Curt can never fill the Obinze-sized hole in Ifemelu's heart, but a once-impoverished existence suddenly distends with luxury, almost to glut. Kayaking, fancy restaurants, loft apartments. The shock written on the faces of others upon hearing of the relationship seems like a small price to pay for the alleviation of the psychic burden that attends poverty.

I used to joke with Mom that we could reconcile my wanting to be a writer with my marrying into a rich family. What went unsaid between us was that marrying rich always seemed to mean marrying white.

As is the tendency of white men, Curt's gaze exoticizes Ifemelu. His enchantment at the way she enlists her entire body in the task of laughter, his breathless, post-coital confession of never having slept with a Black woman before, the exhibitionism with which he seems eager to show her off—his Black girlfriend, his African girlfriend.

I was never in Katherine's head, but it's difficult to imagine that I was ever her African boyfriend. We certainly weren't steeped enough in the terminology at the time to recognize it as anything like that. As children sometimes interact with each other absent the prejudice they learn from their parents or from TV, so did we glide through our romance absent racial and ethnographic prejudice. Our ingenue-ity explains some of why I never felt exoticized with her, but another piece of the puzzle lies within the gender dynamics at work.

Against the backdrop of a globally patriarchal super-
structure, it is so much easier for men to "other" women,
to objectify them, to imbue in them, or their vision of
them, their own pathologies, than it is for women writ
large to do with men. That isn't to say I never had a
girlfriend who called me her Black Panther or who
indulged in behavior I had to put a swift stop to. It is
only to say that it is easily understood why Ifemelu had
a harder time than I did.

Sylvia Wynter, in her 2003 essay, "Unsettling the
Coloniality of Being/Power/Truth/Freedom," writes
about what Aníbal Quijano called the "Racism/Ethni-
cism complex," which Walter Mignolo acknowledges as
the "foundational colonial difference" upon which the
world of modernity was constructed:

> This seeing that if, as Quijano rightly insists,
> race—unlike gender (which has a biogenetically
> determined anatomical differential correlate onto
> which each culture's system of gendered oppositions
> can be anchored)—is a purely invented construct
> that has no such correlate, it was this construct that
> would enable the now globally expanding West
> to replace the earlier mortal/immortal, natural/
> supernatural, human/the ancestors, the gods/God

distinction as the one on whose basis all human groups had millennially "grounded" their descriptive statement/prescriptive statements of what it is to be human, and to reground its secularizing own on a newly projected human/subhuman distinction instead. That is, on Quijano's "Racism/Ethnicism" complex, Winant's "race concept," Mignolo's "colonial difference," redefined in the terms of the Spanish state's theoretical construct of a "by-nature difference" between Spaniards and the indigenous peoples of the Americas: a difference defined in Ginés de Sepúlveda's sixteenth-century terms as almost a difference between "monkeys and men," homunculi and true humans. "Race" was therefore to be, in effect, the non-supernatural but no less extrahuman ground (in the reoccupied place of the traditional ancestors/gods, God, ground) of the answer that the secularizing West would now give to the Heideggerian question as to the who, and the what we are.[5] (Citations omitted)

More simply, race—that externalized pulverizing of the multi-faceted mosaic of ethnicity—becomes the methodology through which the other is dehumanized. Dehumanized as made less than human, dehumanized as made more than human. It is how women of color are made into objects and their male counterparts beasts of burden. It is how women of color are imagined as the ever-untiring saviors of The American Republic and their male counterparts demi-gods capable of other-worldly sexual prowess. The lived experience of the orientalized is obliterated in the face of "Black people are really good at sex." "If she laughs like that, I wonder how she does *other* things." Fanon writes, in *Black Skin, White Masks*: "The simplicity of the Negro is a myth created by superficial observers."[6]

Still, Fanon's characterization of Black men loving white women as an attempt at self-actualization through the attainment of whiteness strikes me as simplistic. Maybe it isn't for some, maybe it is the whole of their truth that they see all of civilization trapped between white breasts.

Many heterosexual, cisgendered Black men such as myself are questioned often and vociferously about their pursuit of white women, particularly in the context of American history, a context that includes the lynching of Emmett Till, where the mere rumor of amorous relations could lead to the most obscene of deaths for a Black 14-year-old boy. "Look what they've done to us in their name," people would say of white women, as though the present-day biracial coupling were a betrayal of the cosmic order. And the plaintiveness deepens when one considers the deplorable treatment America gives to African-American women on a second-by-second basis. One need look no further than the maternal mortality rates to see a country that views these women as not just disposable but disgusting. Not only are Black men leaving, they are marrying into the oppressor class. And behind them, the howls and recriminations: "they'll never accept you; you'll never be like them; you're still just a nigger to them."

This is the stereotype. The reality, in this present day, is riddled with complication, not the least of which is the very argument that loving who you love is a political choice as much as it is anything else. We see the demographic vote totals from the 2016 presidential election and the 2018 midterms. We see who chose Beto, and we see who chose Ted Cruz. We see who chose Doug Jones, and we see who chose Roy Moore. (In that last contest, Black women remained praised and not-listened-to.) The reality is that, very often, white women will be the subject of ridicule when they intrude upon the fruits of Black creativity, while in other sectors, they remain the Holy Grail for men of color, whether consciously or unconsciously. And, still, there is so much more at work. There is environment, nurture, who you surround yourself with, your workplace, your commute, your spin class, your temporary homelessness, and those instances when you're able to mock those people in spin class, infinite opportunities for kismet. There is who hurt you, who, in your past, had the volcanic temper, who preferred chaos to peace. There is whether you like that or not. There is context.

When two people marry and one of them is Black, who will give The Talk to their children? And will the non-Black partner truly understand the urgency behind it? At the end of the day, people who look like her are not automatically endangered any time a police officer is near.

But so much of this feels like discourse I'm a dance-step away from. The racialization of gender in America vis-a-vis whites projecting onto Blacks is a thing that has affected and will continue to affect me, for as long as I remain within America's national borders and wherever I encounter vestiges of American empire abroad. But it is as though I am arriving halfway through the movie. There was so much I needed to learn, so much catching-up to do. At the bottom of it all, I wanted not to feel guilty. I wanted the act of loving a white woman and letting her love me not to be a betrayal of cosmic order.

I wanted to write off my comfort with them as inconsequential and not evidence of more insidious impulses. Because trailing me was the question that would haunt me well into adulthood, love no longer a passive thing that happened to me but now a verb, something you did to someone: did I prefer them?

Brown Sugar Days

I spent the fiftieth anniversary of Bloody Sunday in Paris.

It is a historical quirk just how many Bloody Sundays there are, how often the theme occurs, of bloodletting on what is ostensibly supposed to be a peaceful day, a day of rest. A macrocosmic display of human failure, angels hovering in the sky with their flaming swords while we monkeys carve each other in two. Four Bloody Sundays came as a result of British dominion (or attempts thereat) over Ireland, two of them barely a year apart. There's the 1905 St. Petersburg massacre that led to the Russian Revolution. In 1923 in Sydney on Cape Breton Island in Nova Scotia, steelworkers aiming for union recognition provoked the ire of mounted police who chased down and struck women and children. Residents of Bydgoszcz, Poland, at the onset of World War II, saw their own Bloody Sunday in 1939.

A Bloody Sunday is the culmination of a polity spinning against the way it turns. Contain a sin, Original or otherwise, for long enough in one's chest, and paroxysms begin to wrack the heart. Arteries and veins begin to calcify, blood has a harder time getting where it needs to go, so too does oxygen. The body politic dements.

Such is America's Bloody Sunday: March 7, 1965.

John Lewis (who would later become a Congressman) of the SNCC, Reverend Hosea Williams of the SCLC, Bob Mants of the SNCC, and Albert Turner of the SCLC led nearly 600 protesters in this first leg of the Selma-to-Montgomery marches of 1965. That morning, the marchers walked along U.S. Highway 80, southeast out of Selma, Alabama. They came to the Edmund Pettus Bridge, at the other end of which stood County Sheriff Jim Clark and all the young, bloodthirsty white men he'd deputized overnight to deal with what appeared in their gaze to be a looming Negro Menace. After a few perfunctory calls to turn back, the white lawmen beat the protesters bloody while cameras filmed and broadcast the carnage into millions of American living rooms.

The occasion, like so many episodes of bloodletting, whether broadcast over television or splashed above the folds of newspapers, pushed the battle for civil rights forward. If enough whites could be seen as deplorable in the eyes of enough other whites, then perhaps some acknowledgement could be made for how the worst of them had worked to systematize oppression and how the less horrible of them had become complicit in it. Bodies quite literally thrown on the gears in an attempt to stop the machine.

By the time the fiftieth anniversary of this day arrived, America had a Black president. "Summary: President Obama and the First Family joined thousands of Americans in Selma, Alabama to honor the sacrifice and bravery of the men and women who bled there in 1965, in support of voting rights for all African Americans"[7] reads the sub-heading of the White House's archived page. There's a photo on the page of President Obama, holding hands with John Lewis and an elderly woman who had endured white hatred on that bridge with him 50 years prior. Michelle Obama is there at the front, as are Barack and Michelle's daughters, Sasha and Malia. You can see a bit of Reverend Al Sharpton's head over President Obama's shoulder, and somewhere in there, according to the photo's caption, are former President George W. Bush and his wife Laura.

On the same day President Obama would give one of the great speeches of his presidency, I found myself in the art deco Rex Theatre on Boulevard Poissonière in Paris's 2nd Arrondissement. What brought me to Paris was a dual degree program between Columbia Law School, which I was attending at the time, and Sciences Po's law school in Paris. Rather than spend my third and final year of law school in New York City, a place I had come to loathe, I would live in Paris, attending courses as part of a bilingual program of study, and emerge with two degrees for the price of one. (If you're wondering what the downside was, there was no downside.) So March 7, 2015 sees me in Paris, a month away from the end of my semester, two months away from my return to the States, in the midst of the most charmed quarter-year of my life, celebrating the first annual Brown Sugar Days film festival: a program of five African-American films, starting with the acclaimed Sundance darling *Dear White People* and ending with *The Best Man Holiday*, sequel to the seminal 1999 film *The Best Man*. Between the posters scattered throughout Paris and the web advertisements, the day was marketed very much as a Taye Diggs extravaganza. But it ended up a wonderful marathon featuring a revolving door of familiar faces like Sanaa Lathan, Regina Hall, Morris Chestnut, Gabrielle Union and others.

Other than *Dear White People*, all of the films were in French, for the benefit of the almost exclusively French audience. Because *DWP* was, that day, celebrating its European premiere, Justin Simien, the director, appeared afterwards for a transatlantic Q&A. The discourse between Black French (mostly) women and a Black American man was an iteration of a discussion I'd had before, illustrative of the pervasiveness of questions about sexuality, police brutality, and campus racism. We were in the throes of our first Black President's second term in office, I and my fellow expats at the festival. We had time and space for this.

It was serendipitous watching *Dear White People* in that moment because the film operated for me and for many of my friends back home very much like biography: Black students making a go of it within a majority-white student population, trying to assimilate or fight back, with a cast of very recognizable archetypes (the revolutionary, the Black girl with the blond wigs and the blue-eyes, the Oofta who modulates his Blackness depending on his audience, the gay nerd who fits in nowhere, the mixed-race, those engaged in inter-racial couples, etc.). I saw in that film my experience and the experiences of nearly all of my friends of color, both in college and in law school. Seeing that film in a 2500-seat theater filled almost exclusively with Black people suffused the air with an almost overwhelming sense of rightness. I'd never really, truly had anything like this, and yet I knew then and there that this is how things should be.

The other films were more traditional fare, rom-coms (particularly the *Think Like a Man* series) made by Blacks, featuring Blacks, for Blacks. With references it was expected (perhaps rightly) that only we expats would get, and dynamics only we expats would appreciate, and with music that only we expats would hold this close to our hearts.

Still, those films became participatory in a way I don't think I fully expected. When Taye Diggs pressed his handwritten sign to the window of that radio station booth, silently asking if Sanaa Lathan would go out with him, and Sanaa Lathan nodded her head "yes," the chorus of young women in the audience shouted "OUIIIIIIIII!" When Taraji P. Henson kissed Michael Ealy during the rooftop dinner that he had prepared as part of a project to woo her, the audience erupted in rapturous cheers.

These were pockets of elation in what began as a somewhat tentative and sedate audience, but by the time the DJ started his set, the crowd in the balcony had begun to move. "Hip Hop Hooray" put people's hands in the air, but it took Fat Joe's "Lean Back" to get people out of their seats. The dancehall sprinkled throughout had the girls in the aisle and out of their seats bruking it out, and when the DJ finally spun "Bugatti" by Ace Hood, I had lost myself completely.

It was as though someone had brought Harlem to Paris. There was relaxed hair, natural hair, kinks, curls, nappy hair, straight hair, hair in all varieties, and Menthol cigarette smoke curling in streams that waltzed outside, couples on dates, friends eager to dance and see Taye Diggs on screen, men and women eager to laugh at the comic who skewered and uplifted the Black experience in America and in France. Other than a brief sojourn to the 18th where Paris keeps all its West Africans, this was the highest concentration of Black French people I'd ever experienced in the city.

The day was a magnificent, transcontinental celebration of Blackness. I could not have imagined a better way to commemorate the sacrifice of the marchers on the Selma-to-Montgomery march, the brutality they endured on the Edmund Pettus Bridge. To be loudly and proudly in love with oneself, that seemed, in the afternoon heat, why the Civil Rights Warriors had fought the way they did. That day was about Black love.

All those people in all those seats around me. They were beautiful.

I could look around me in that theater and see potential partners. Yet, at the time, complication persisted. And when I speak of complication, I'm speaking of Leila.

Leila

We met in a class on environmental law. When she spoke, it was with a whisper and rasp.

Like so many of my close friendships, it began with us smoking shisha one night near Les Halles. We'd commiserated through classes together, and she'd grown so adept at noting my tics that she could tell when I was only pretending to understand something I'd heard her say. "T'as compris?" A pause. "Non, j'ai su."

The girl with the whisper-rasp has cancer.

That night we'd first met, she had been coming from the hospital. We were sitting outside in cushioned chairs, passing the pipe between us when she told me, and I stared at her. In my mind, a dark and malignant polyp sat on her larynx and every time I prompted her to speak was a wrong I had committed against her. The wisdom in her reaction was heard rather than seen. Even trying to capture it now in written text, I am unable to communicate that understanding that was communicated to me. To assume that any affliction has, built in its core, the potential for wisdom is to romanticize suffering, to rob it of its harm and its pain, to turn it into something desired. The penitent with whip-scars on her back. No. This wisdom was threaded with kindness. Each husky, throaty word is a reminder that the thing sitting on her larynx is the same thing that kills people I love. But when she closes her mouth, the thing is hidden behind lips bent into a shy smile, fighting against itself.

She showed me photos of herself and her family. In them, her hair was a russet mane. Autumn surrounded her face. When I last saw her, her hair was shorter. Still a royal thing, but it had thinned, and she could no longer grow it to its former length.

The women in the Rex Theatre were possibilities. Leila was my partner.

There is a difference, this time.

This time, I saw faces.

It's tempting to say that I learned to see Black beauty, that I learned to desire kinky hair and skin light as sand and dark as star-dappled night. But perhaps it is more appropriate to say that I unlearned prejudice. Less building a bridge and more breaking down a wall.

When I read *Americanah*, I was jealous that loving a Black person came so naturally to Ifemelu, as though it were a thing that required effort. But Black beauty and the battle to determine what exactly it consisted of were the fabric of her existence from the moment she was born. She was raised in it. I didn't truly see it until I became a man.

Her one true love is Obinze, the learned, worldly Nigerian who endures his own trial-ridden journey to the West and back to Nigeria. That love pushes the story. It is, during much of Ifemelu's time in America, her sole link to her home, and maybe that is the true cause of my envy. I look at Ifemelu in love with Obinze, and I see a woman in love with home, even if it is only, in a sense, the idea of home. It all seems so simple. Even though the love is star-crossed, it feels as though she has it figured out.

Jo

In 2011, I accidentally Facebook-friended someone I would proceed to have a crush on for two years, someone whose voice I would not hear until the summer of 2013, almost two years after we'd first "met," when I watched her give a speech on YouTube from my laptop at work in the West Bank.

She accepted my friend request on July 12, 2011. During the rest of that summer, every time she "liked" a Facebook status of mine, or shared a link I'd posted, or tweeted back at me, my heart did a triple axel. I started reading Joan Didion and Zadie Smith to impress her. We were both writers. She was in law school. I would be starting the following year.

For the two years between when we first "met" and when we finally found ourselves in the same room, I worried that she would forever remain a picture of a young woman. A funny tweet, an enthusiastic Facebook post, an excerpt from a poem on Tumblr.

When I watched her give that speech on YouTube, she sounded exactly as I had imagined she would sound. A triumph of imagination on my part, maybe. But I had heard that voice before. The linked post, the Facebook message, the tweet. Each was a trill that formed the grand melody of her. So, when she finally spoke, flesh and blood and soul, it was less revelation than confirmation.

That crush morphed into a friendship that has enriched my life beyond measure. But I'll never forget how it started. Me clicking through a comment on a friend's Facebook post, traveling at the speed of light to her profile, and, upon seeing her face, having the breath snatched from my lungs.

Jo was American Black, radiantly so. And I was smitten. No, not smitten. Decapitated.

Nee

In December 2010, my second semester of film school, my ninth month sober, I met Nee. Our class is gathered together to watch her act out a four-page play I'd written about an author who realizes that, in order to win the Hugo Award for Best Novel, she must kill off her protagonist and end her bestselling 12-book franchise.

November 18, 2016, almost six years to the month, I've come to see her star in a play at Playwrights Horizons. She doesn't know I'm coming, so when she sees me in the building's elevator prior, the sunshine in her eyes and the way we embrace seem to signal something more fervent, more eager, than the platonic. Dinner follows at the West Bank Café with her co-stars.

Towards the end of the night, we're preparing to leave. I've just emerged from the bathroom to see her from behind, arms stretched before her, holding my attaché case. Her hair is dark and curly and unfurling away from her face. In the memory, her top is pink and orange together. Sherbet.

On the Metro-North train ride back home, I discover, over text, that, for years now, we've nursed crushes on each other.

Never in my wildest dreams.

We saw so much theater together, she the actress, me the playwright.

The next month, December, Nee took me to see *Rancho Viejo*, which was opening at Playwrights Horizons. The play did not feel three hours long. We were partnered with her co-star from "A Life," Marinda, and Marinda's beau. The playwright for the play both Nee and Marinda had starred in was a few rows ahead of us, on an edge seat. The row we occupied seemed to have been reserved specifically for the cast of that play.

Before the play, Nee had scooped me up at a nearby Starbucks and we'd proceeded to the venue where someone official commandeered us for several photos before the Opening Night backdrop. After the play, Nee flitted through the crowds both upstairs and in the downstairs lobby, flashing what a pensioner the previous Sunday had, with no small amount of admiration, told me was her megawatt smile, and talking about the play we'd just seen and the play she'd just finished starring in.

Across the street was a private party for the show. After we divested ourselves of our bags and Nee had already been accosted by several admirers, we sought out a table of familiars, landing finally among her cast-mates and the playwright.

The evening was keyed to a glorious pitch by animated conversation—me and Adam Bock about writing novels and writing plays, me and my similarly situated partner admiring the tableau we were witnessing, Adam and his cast members rejoicing over their write-up in the *New York Times*.

Thursday, January 12 of the following year, my attempt at a birthday gift: I brought Nee to the BAM theater for a production of Martin McDonagh's "Beauty Queen of Leenane." My first semester at Tisch, a friend inducted me into the Church of McDonagh after noting my adoration of "The Pillowman" and my subsequent head-over-heels infatuation with "The Lieutenant of Inishmore." When I'd first seen that tickets to "Beauty Queen" were available and that, for maybe the first time in my life, I could afford to buy theater tickets in something approaching the spur of the moment, and noting that Nee's availability coincided with her birthday weekend, I purchased away.

She hadn't seen much McDonagh before that night and gushed at length about the play during our later promenade.

It didn't have the feel of a send-off then, but the more time passes, the thicker the cloak of finality that seems to have appeared in the interim. A stage play has bookended the whole thing.

It is the fall of 2016. We're having brunch, and we'll soon be running late for her last day. Her play is closing. And there is something just beyond the edge of reality that I glimpse when I see her face inclined towards the napkin she's placing on her lap, something beyond the realm of the concrete and corporeal, something beyond even truth, that collapses past and future into the present, and that prompts me to whisper beneath my breath, in awe, that no one can possibly be that beautiful.

* * *

Nee was American Black. You could hear the honey in her voice. When I think of Black love, I often think of her. Uniting Nee and me was a voracious love of theater, a deep and abiding appreciation for a singular art form. Storytelling joined us. And we were both of this country.

It is destructive but perhaps inevitable to project the questions that dog an individual person onto a romantic relationship, that working-out of the self, but I think of Nee and I think of that question I had so feared asking earlier: did I prefer them? Was I simply more comfortable with white partners? Was it easier for me to imagine futures with women a different color than my family?

I think of Jo, and I think of the Rex Theatre, and I think of Nee, and I wonder if all the rest was me simply turning against the way I spun. Miniature Bloody Sundays where corporeal desire battled with contextualized desire, id versus superego, and I became a two-headed beast savaging its own self. It is not failure for a Black man to love a woman who isn't Black. Still, that truth does nothing to abate the feeling of rightness that attended those moments of what I feel comfortable now calling "Black love."

PART 4

ABSOLUTE ZERO

The Minute You Step Outside

The other character who helps immerse Ifemelu in American culture is Blaine. It seems as though Ifemelu's journey to and through America was always fated to be a temporary affair. This is made clear in the beginning with her wishing, planning, to leave Blaine and go back home. But it lends those portions of the book set in Maryland and in New Haven the air of, not necessarily summer holiday, but a gap year. This is study abroad. Which is maybe an unfair characterization. For many immigrants, the journey is (meant to be) permanently one-way. There's a finality to that initial leavetaking.

This is part of the complex braid of reasons why Ifemelu never fully commits to becoming American Black. The gaze is always too anthropological.

Oddly enough, what seems to push Ifemelu deeper into American-ness is her breakup with Curt and her subsequent relationship with Blaine.

Her time with Curt is blanketed in a kind of charmed insouciance. I read the book in the summer before my year in Paris, but, returning to it now, I see so much of my sojourn in the City of Lights in Ifemelu's relationship with Curt. They exist apart from the world, blanketed in a kind of divine providence that molds the universe to Curt's wishes. When Ifemelu is told at the spa by an Asian woman that she cannot get her eyebrows done because they are "too curly," a simple call from Curt is all it takes to pummel the desk attendant into obsequious submission. Coating the two of them almost like an invisibility cloak is the easing of worry that wealth provides. For many who have never had much money before, or who find themselves in a near-constant state of attending to the costs of living, the ultimate enchantment of money is not the simple having of it, but the alleviation of worry. When you can reach a state where a bill in the mail or in your inbox is not cause for worry—that is the allure. Curt and Ifemelu exist several stages past this—their world is lofts and family restaurants and fundraising events where Ifemelu is exoticized. Curt understands the soft racism enough for the two to commiserate, but not well enough to see many of its other manifestations. ("It was not that they avoided race, she and Curt. They talked about it in the slippery way that admitted nothing and engaged nothing and ended with the word 'crazy,' like a curious nugget to be examined and then put aside. Or as jokes that left her with a small and numb discomfort that she never admitted to him."[1]) Wealth lowers the stakes. Even though its forcefield can never fully protect one from racism—structural or personal—it grants apartness. Not godhood but stacks of greenbacks carry you into the firmament from whence you can gaze upon the rest of us scurrying around like ants.

At a dinner party, some years into her time with Blaine and a day after Barack Obama has become the Democratic Party's candidate in the 2008 election for President of the United States, a white man proclaims that Obama will end racism in America—not an uncommon sentiment among both white and Black Americans at the time. Even one of America's foremost essayists, Ta-Nehisi Coates, admits to being drawn into the fantasy of racial progress, letting the wool of audacious hope obscure the clear-eyed cynicism that had served him for so long.

Ifemelu counters that this a lie and details her experience coming from Nigeria, where race isn't an issue, and how she only became Black once she landed in America. "The words had, once again, overtaken her, they overpowered her throat, and tumbled out."[2] And suddenly, she's talking about being Black and being in love with a white man and how "'[w]hen you are black in America and you fall in love with a white person, race doesn't matter when you're alone together because it's just you and your love. But the minute you step outside, race matters. But we don't talk about it. We don't even tell our white partners the small things that piss us off and the things we wish they understood better, because we're worried they will say we're overreacting or we're being too sensitive."[3]

What prompts Ifemelu to start her blog is one of those episodes that an uncharitable, outside observer might characterize as an unfair enlargement of a misunderstanding. Curt flips through an issue of *Essence* and comments on how the magazine is "racially skewed"[4] for featuring only Black women. I've seen and heard this happen enough times to recognize the tectonic anger Ifemelu must have had to suppress in order to turn this into a proper teachable moment for her boyfriend at the time. She takes him to a bookstore and drags him through two thousand pages of women's magazines, asking Curt to count how many Black women he sees. Their final tally: three. "'Or, maybe four.'"[5] Ifemelu details how all the beauty advice in these columns, all the advertised products, every valorization of beauty, is meant for women much whiter than her. This is the context in which a magazine like *Essence* exists. Curt's response: "'Okay, babe, okay. I didn't mean for it to be such a big deal[.]'"[6]

Ifemelu drafts a lengthy letter to Wambui, the "firm voice" from the classroom discussion on *Roots* and the word "nigger," and who has subsequently become a close friend, and tells her about the "bookstore, the magazines, the things she didn't tell Curt, things unsaid and unfinished."

Wambui's reaction is supportive. She is Curt's diametric opposite. Rather than belittle Ifemelu's objections, she says, "'This is so raw and true. More people should read this. You should start a blog.'"[7] She does not know the stratospheric rise the blog will bring about in Ifemelu's life, nor does she know how the endeavor would propel her into her next relationship, how it would thrust her deeper into the question of American Blackness, and how it would position her, where it would place her, as the country readied to elect its first Black president.

If Ifemelu's time in America is study abroad and language immersion, the blog is where she practices her vocabulary. Language is the conduit of life experience, and articulation enhances experience. It is a deepening. Things have the potential to come at you in high definition.

As with so many episodes of self-improvement in my life, I learned the vocabulary of American Blackness not in classrooms but in school nonetheless. In this respect, Ifemelu and I are twinned. Blaine is a professor at Yale. The man I style as my big brother, one of my closest friends, and the man to hurl me into the deep end of American Blackness, was a fellow Yale student. His name was Jonathan.

Piano Lessons

In my second semester of college, I played the role of Doaker in a production of August Wilson's "The Piano Lesson." My friend and director, Jon—an upperclassmen then, now the artistic director of a theater in Rhode Island— drafted me for the role of a man almost three decades my senior because of my prodigious beard-growing abilities, a mutant power I inherited from my father. I had performed in theater in high school, but it was a collection of alien experiences. I was a chorus member in "Agamemnon," and LeBret in "Cyrano de Bergerac"—a Greek and a Frenchman. This role, more than anything, was pressed upon me, and I've nothing but boundless thanks for this friend, in part because I will never understand his insistence, though I benefited so much from it. The play is set in 1936 Pittsburgh and focuses on the Charles family, of which Doaker is the patriarch. In the Charles household is a piano that has served as an heirloom and whose fraught history is unearthed as the play progresses. On it is carved the faces of a young slave and the slave's mother, pieces of property who were sold by a plantation owner whose wife subsequently grew morose in their absence.

In a scene towards the middle of the play, I entertain old friends around a living room table with a jug of whiskey, and we get to talking about a place called Parchman's Farm. Back in 2006, during rehearsals and even during tech week, that place was only a pair of words I had to memorize, embedded in the immediate context of the performance. But during the sharing of old stories, the men fall into song, and they begin singing "O, Berta." The shotglasses become instruments, a palm slams on the table to keep the beat, and they sing. Eventually old, curmudgeonly Doaker gets roped in, asking Berta not to marry a farmin' man but to marry a railroad man instead, and we made music with that table, and it was only a glimpse, but I saw the hammer hit the rail spike and I saw the sweat soak the shirt of the convict in front of me, and I saw a man, in the break between beats, run his forearm across his brow, and I was there. On that chain gang in Mississippi. On Parchman's Farm. Then the song finished.

And I'm left wondering what miracle of time travel sent me back there.

How many moments of simultaneous transfiguration did August Wilson write into that scene? The song induced a trance then as it does now. And in the singing, one gets to dreaming. I hear that song now and sometimes I think I am among the delivered, on the other side of the parted Red Sea. Sometimes I wonder if perhaps all I need do is move a few inches to feel the chains around my ankles. Sometimes I wonder if I've forgotten the hammer in my hands. If I've forgotten that I'm still in the midst of building someone else's railroad.

That song was bled into existence. Outside the confines of that vision, when Doaker and Lymon and Boy Willie and Wining Boy finish laying down that track of rail, when they head back to their cells, did they hear hymns on the way? "Amazing Grace"? "Blessed Assurance"? Did that prison population include home-grown ministers who advised a New Testament restraint, or was the faith carried among that population a faith that God would serve as the architect of their revenge? In churches in Harlem, Virginia, and Mississippi, when Black ministers speak to Black congregations in the abstract, the language is decoded, and uniting the specifics of each personal trial, each tribal tribulation, is the conviction that God is not sleeping, that it is only a matter of time before the Good Lord manages them all, before the locusts and the frogs and the water turned to blood.

The sermon is the song and the song is the sermon. Deliverance from bondage is the promise. And the Black American looks to the example of the Israelite, looks to the example of the promise fulfilled, and wonders when will it be her turn. When will it be his?

Magical Negro

I don't remember speaking with my mother about Barack Obama first announcing his candidacy. She might have made glancing references to Jesse Jackson, whose last shot at the Presidency went wide of the mark a year after I was born. I don't know that she ever took him seriously; I don't know that she didn't. But I do know that the genre of respectability politics that lurks in the lizard part of the immigrant's brain saw in Barack Obama an idealized son. Mom bought his memoir, and it was no secret that she intended for the future President and me to share that affinity that fills the air between those men of color who walk the halls of the Ivy League.

A place like Yale operates in a way that made the isolation effect of massive wealth familiar to me. It ensconces. It protects. It's the bubble, the gown in fraught town-gown relations. It becomes the bit on the resume that will make getting the next job much easier, it becomes the talking point with the hiring partner at the law firm, it becomes the annual Harvard-Yale tailgate, a single syllable whispered like a password through the keyholes of life. I knew even then that I was sitting in classes with people who would run Fortune 500 companies. Indeed, less than a decade later, many of them would appear on the Forbes 30 Under 30 List, their first of what I'm sure will be many bouts of recognition. I knew that I was having dinner and chatting "about last night" with a future Senator, maybe even for my state, or, at the very least, a state rep. They would do things like cross the Antarctic and work at *The*

New Yorker and get elected and write award-winning memoirs. They would found startups, they would give speeches at South by Southwest, opening for Obama. They would win Grammys.

I was privileged, though. Not necessarily by socio-economic status. Since sixth grade, I had been the son of a widow, a son who, with his siblings, helped his mother clean office buildings to pay bills. Despite what opponents of affirmative action might claim, I was certainly not privileged by my skin color; I still lived in a country that, even in the midst of Obama's ascent, was more accustomed to thinking of Black people as things (concrete and abstract) rather than people. But I was privileged in one regard: I had gone to a private boarding school for four years.

At Choate Rosemary Hall, I learned not only about Palestinians and Israelis but about forging relationships with professors to smooth the way for recommendation letters later on. I learned what Office Hours were, and that some professors preferred to be pestered outside of class—indeed, saw it as evidence of commitment to the course. It helped that I lived in the same building as a lot of these people, that we shared a campus, that the man who taught English also barked orders at us on the football field. It becomes easier to see a professor as someone to take things from when you can ask them about trouble you're having with both a girl and a grade. I also learned the difference between rich and wealthy, and I learned to be comfortable in cavernous homes where each child had their own monogrammed towels and washcloths. I learned to understand summer and winter as verbs. But I also learned about warrant and belonging. I learned how to walk like I owned the place.

I wasn't an extraordinary high school student but I was better than good, and everyone knew me. My winding up at Yale, many people told me after, was a foregone conclusion. It wasn't so dramatic as prophecy fulfilled; it was more pedestrian cosmology. It was the changing of the seasons.

I assumed I knew who Barack was. We were the same color. By dint of academic pedigree, he was exceptional. So was I.

* * *

Much has been written about Barack Obama's macrocosmic efforts at unity. There's his famous "Red America, Blue America" speech at the Democratic National Convention. There was his (self-)presentation as America's absolution for its Original Sin. His coming heralded a new era. It wasn't quite the end of history but a sort

of end to American History. We could go about forgetting or no longer worrying about the pesky business of
systemic racism, of the legacy of slavery and Redemp-
tion and Jim Crow, of the bill America had run up in its
plunder of Black wealth, tangible and intangible.

But happening at the same time were the microcosmic uniting and holding-together of relationships. I
wonder at the families, formerly estranged, that were
reunited by the man's promise. I wonder at the couples,
like Ifemelu and Blaine, who remained together to see
this one out: to see, first if he could do it, get elected;
and, later, to see if he could last all four, then eight years
without having his gray matter spilled onto the back-
seats of a convertible ambling down a downtown Dallas
street. I wonder at the people sitting on the couch
watching the results come in together. Maybe the lights
are off in the house, and the only glow comes from the
television. Maybe one or the other is on the road, obsessively refreshing Twitter or checking the count through
a livestream. Maybe they gather or huddle together in a
ballroom, a tiny collection of atoms forming an anxious
molecule, trembling with anxiety and, dare they say,
hope. Friends, foes, fuck-buddies. Family.

Ifemelu is, at first, skeptical. She prefers Hillary
Clinton's square trouser suits, "her face a mask of

resolve, her prettiness disguised".[8] But one day, she picks up Barack Obama's memoir, *Dreams From My Father*, and consumes the whole thing in a day and a half, while listening to Nina Simone on Blaine's iPod speaker. The result is electric:

> He reminded her of Obinze's expression for people he liked. *Obi ocha.* A clean heart. She believed Barack Obama. When Blaine came home, she sat at the dining table, watching him chop fresh basil in the kitchen, and said "If only the man who wrote this book could be the president of America."
>
> Blaine's knife stopped moving. He looked up, eyes lit, as though he had not dared hope she would believe the same thing that he believed, and she felt between them the first pulse of a shared passion.[9]

* * *

I remember where I was when it was announced that Barack Obama would be the 44th President of the United States of America. I was in a Berkeley common room with my drinking buddies and their friends. Someone popped champagne. Those white friends of mine who'd canvassed for him in places like Ohio were crying, and so I wept with them. It's what you're supposed to do when you're living through history, right? I wonder who kissed and didn't think about how they might regret it the morning after, who coupled, who called whom and confessed or forgave, who saw this as a finish line—not for a fundamentally broken America in the process of healing, but for a relationship they'd hoped would last long enough for this moment.

I used to think I could take credit for the Barack Obama campaign poster in our family living room and the Obama/Biden '08 buttons in our photo cabinet. My siblings and I had all been sent to prestigious American schools, some of the most illustrious schools in the country, whose names rang bells around the world. My youngest sister and I shared an alma mater with John F. Kennedy. I'd gone to the same college as a few Bushes. I would later attend the same law school as Supreme Court Justice Ruth Bader Ginsburg. And in all these places, we, Mom's progeny, conducted our own romances across color lines, experienced our own personal race-based slights, witnessed the ways in which our color-mates moved or were kept from moving through the world. In these places, thrust together with American Blacks, we completed whatever transformation we'd begun at the moment of our birth on American soil.

With each vacation or weekend spent home, we carried the perfume of our contemporaries. We filled the house with it. Our music, our *Chappelle's Show* jokes, our vocabulary. And after we'd left, Mom would walk through what lingered.

By virtue of birthright, we were American citizens and, thus, inheritors of America's legacy. Not only that, we were charged with charting its future.

We'd done it. We'd become American Black. We'd stretched the elastic of that identity to fit our bodies and accommodate our spirits. Barack Obama made us feel Black in a way nothing else had done before. Of course his magic would affect Mom, right?

* * *

She was already undergoing her own transformation.

The church to which we migrated during my senior year of high school and at which we stayed through my time in law school was founded in 1635. Ten Colonialists had arrived in Wethersfield, Connecticut the year before, gathered together, and found in the wilderness of that country the presence of a God who could teach these immigrants how to live. The quarter is to this day replete with Colonial architecture, as if each new cycle of development the town has seen has sought to further preserve the place's historical bequest. The shingles, the red of the brick, the height of the achromatic spires. The chill of the sanctuary on a snow-limned February morning.

It was the very first time I'd ever seen a woman minister—lovely and loving, the antithesis of the hell-fire-and-brimstone Baptists I'd grown up in fear of, Old Testament fundamentalists whose God lived in the mountains and hurled commandments and plague with equally indiscriminate wrath. This minister, a Congregationalist, told me once over coffee that church was more than a building or a denomination. It was catholic, small *c*. It was Matthew 18:20: "For where two or three are gathered in my name, there I am in the midst of them."

This church fixed our leaky roof. It corralled our wayward loved ones. It smiled genuinely. It took us out for pizza. It cooked for Mom and the rest of us.

When, during my college and graduate school years, I would come home for a weekend or for vacation and accompany Mom to her early Sunday morning Bible Study group, and we would discuss James Chapter 4, I felt I was sitting with the salt of the earth. We were in this together, fumbling our way forward, trying to figure out the balance between submitting oneself to God's will and acting with agency.

These were Mom's constant companions while her children were away at school, emptying the nest. We were among the only congregants of color, but this reaching across the color line seemed to be exactly the thing Barack Obama was referencing whenever he invoked this inchoate unity that some of us, eyes swollen nearly shut with all the wounding America had done to us, had so much trouble seeing.

I think these white Americans shared DNA with those with whom I would later celebrate Obama's win. These were the white Americans who would cheer alongside Mom, who would rejoice, despite their different histories and the different motives those histories had spawned.

And then there were Mom's colleagues from work, some of them African-American, with whom she would spend time. I will never know what it is like to be a widow, but I do know loneliness and I do know how much of a blessing the thirst-slaking draught of company can be for a parched throat. I imagine Mom picking up her own slang, broadening her own vocabulary, trying it out when she sends us text messages.

So, Election Day comes, then the night when polls close and results come in and Ifemelu is watching with Blaine, who has made virgin cocktails for the friends in attendance. There's Araminta, holding two phones, the quintessential Afropolitan. There's Grace, there's Michael, Paula, Pee, and Nathan. *"If he wins Indiana and Pennsylvania, then that's it. It's looking good in Florida. The news from Iowa is conflicting."*[10]

After Keith Olbermann, "the voice of a searing, sparkling liberal rage,"[11] tells the audience that Barack Obama is projected to be the next president of the United States of America, Ifemelu receives a text from Dike. Dike, about whose identity she'd so often worried. Dike, the wayward child, such a mystery to his mother Aunty Uju. Would he grow up feeling more African or feeling more African-American? In some fashion, the answer is in that text.

"I can't believe it. My president is Black like me."[12]

We bought in. All of us—Mom with her persistent loyalty to Nigerian cuisine, adopting a political posture that demands an accounting for the litany of wrongs perpetrated against African Americans; her children, born and raised with people who looked like us, whose histories were different, but whose futures were now joined together—we all bought in.

It still carries a hint of mystery, of magic, how immigrants can be folded into the identity of so specific a people as African Americans.

But it's the second law of thermodynamics: two initially isolated systems in separate but nearby regions of space, each in equilibrium with itself but not with each other, interacting, fumbling, questing, reaching, eventually, a mutual thermodynamic equilibrium.

PART 5

HOMEGOING

Magnificent Ruin

Ultimately, Ifemelu goes back.

She leaves America. She leaves behind Blaine and Barack Obama; she leaves behind Dike. Her true love, her truth, is back in Lagos. Only there can she be matched to the frequency that sets the tuning fork in her heart aquiver.

The speedboat was gliding on foaming water, past beaches of ivory sand, and trees a bursting, well-fed green. Ifemelu was laughing. She caught herself in mid-laughter, and looked at her present, an orange life jacket strapped around her, a ship in the graying distance, her friends in their sunglasses, on their way to Priye's friend's beach house, where they would grill meat and race barefoot. She thought: I'm really home. I'm home.[1]

A vertiginous paragraph!

There is, of course, the adjustment period, where Lagos, at first, assaults the senses. It's too bright, too loud, but possibility thrums in the air. A violent possibility. You could be the victim of an armed robbery. A stone could turn into a bag of cell phones. Much changes in nine years. Mobiles are ubiquitous where, before, they were the province of the wealthy. The bus conductors have changed their cryptic code into something unrecognizable. Ifemelu must relearn how to move through the city.

But her reentry is smoothed because she is coming back to a rarefied Lagos. Ranyinudo picks her up from the airport, Ranyinudo with the "luxurious, womanly slowness to her gait, a lift, a roll, a toggle of her buttocks with each step."[2] Ifemelu calls it "[a] Nigerian walk. A walk, too, that hinted at excess, as though it spoke of something in need of toning down."[3] Lagos is indeed a city of too much. Too much wealth beside too much poverty, steam rising from too many people crammed together roving through streets with too many potholes, and in the air they all breathe, too many mosquitoes.

At first, it's almost too much, and Ifemelu, on Rany-inudo's bed in the midst of a too-sudden invasion of humidity, feels "guiltily grateful that she had a blue American passport in her bag. It shielded her from choicelessness."[4]

Guilt never goes away, it just finds a new host. Ifemelu is overjoyed to be back, overjoyed in the way that celebrates the place and notices its faults without wholly wishing them away. She and Dike talk, he curious about her new life and the fact that she has a driver who takes her to work, about how the people dressed for church look, "from far away, like flowers in the wind."[5]

Dike eventually comes to Nigeria, auspiciously the day after Ifemelu quits her job to start another blog. Some habits never die, only zombify. The new blog, *The Small Redemptions of Lagos*, fills her with "sanguine expectations."[6] It bears a photograph of an abandoned colonial house on its masthead. Magnificent ruin.

She complains about returnees who complain about Nigeria, making an elaborate metaphor of pani-ni-crafting and food allergies. "It is a nation of people who eat beef and chicken and cow skin and intestines and dried fish in a single bowl of soup, and it is called assorted, so get over yourselves and realize that the way of life here is just that, assorted."[7]

Even her initial reunion with Obinze, who has since married and fathered a child, jars. Obinze, having endured so many indignities in London, having failed to "make it" in England, emerges from a Range Rover like larva turned butterfly. He is a man others praise when he enters the room, even though it still makes him uncomfortable. But he has grown accustomed to the sight of his friends' middle-class beer bellies. He owns property in Dubai. He sometimes longs, in the way of the wealthy, for a romanticized past where "we would heat the iron on the stove when NEPA took light. And how [Okwudiba's] neighbor downstairs used to shout 'Praise the Lord!' whenever the light came back and how even for me there was something so beautiful about the light coming back, when it's out of your control because you don't have a generator."[8]

Ifemelu asks him, during their first sustained outing together, why he fell out of love with America, once his Promised Land.

I realized I could buy America, and it lost its shine. When all I had was my passion for America, they didn't give me a visa, but with my new bank account, getting a visa was very easy. I've visited a few times. I was looking into buying property in Miami. [...] I remember when you first went to Manhattan and you wrote me and said 'It's wonderful but it's not heaven.' I thought of that when I took my first cab ride in Manhattan.[9]

Spoken like a true Afropolitan. And Ifemelu's love bursts through uncertainty into the land of the certain, the assured. She is awake and "eager for tomorrow."[10]

Ifemelu completes the love story. The heroine's journey complicates her, but, in the end, she is returned to the love she had hoped to keep and once thought lost forever. She gets what she wants; the important part being that it is, indeed, what she wants. But love never happens in a vacuum.

During the colonial period, there is the metropole and there is the periphery. Some of this geographic dynamic persists post-colonially, but during the colonial period in particular, it defined spaces and the people kept in them. To cross from one to the other bore implications for your place in society, for your race, your faith, your money, your power. France, not a city in itself but rather a container of the varieties on the urban ideal, is the metropole for Francophone Africa and for the Caribbean. England, with London at its aspirational center, is Anglophone

Africa's metropole. The rest—the colonies—that is periphery.

Hierarchy persists in the periphery: the Martinician is closer to the European exemplar than the African. But modernity wears away at the dynamic.

In an interview with *The Rumpus*, Mohsin Hamid, speaking on his novel *Exit West*, says the following:

> [I]t's not just that the experience of modernity in a city like Lahore, where I live, is becoming like the experience of modernity in large Western cities, but that the experience of modernity in cities like New York, is becoming more like the experience of modernity in Pakistan. In Pakistan, too, we've seen politicians lash out at the judiciary, we've seen questions about whether politicians and their families are enriching themselves. Are political parties true to their principles or simply vehicles for a kind of tribal loyalty? Are elections really reflecting the will of the people? Can we trust our militaries and police to behave in a way which is congruent with democracy? All of these questions that are now coming up in America have been a live thing in Pakistan and much of the world for my entire life. So, the reality is that the experience of democracy

is becoming fraught everywhere. In some places, it's been fraught for a long time.[11]

Everywhere is becoming like America, and America is becoming like everywhere else. In an age of Brexit and an American despot who can destabilize the economy with a tweet, the dream of the West is dissipating. If a Honduran flees to America's southern border seeking asylum, is it because things are so good in America or is it because things are so bad in Tegucigalpa?

A deep dive into American infrastructure reveals roadways in worse shape than some of those potholed embarrassments that plague Lagos. Maternal mortality rates, income inequality, education—the paragons of Western imperialism—slip further each year. When a United States President is laughed at during a meeting at the United Nations, it becomes increasingly difficult to ignore the increasing mockery with which people mention the name of the metropole. Magnificent ruin.

While it may be too early to claim the African Continent is on its way to becoming a global superpower (China may still thwart that ascendance with its own brand of creditor imperialism), its cultural influence grows.

Africa already existed in the traditions transmogrified by slaves into uniquely American rites and ethics and fables and customs. But as the world flattened, connection to the "homeland" became easier and easier. One no longer had to imagine an African Shangri-La; one could see what streets in Togo looked like. One could order ankara prints straight from a shop in West Africa. One could hop onto Google and research just what Easter eggs Beyoncé had sprinkled into her kaleidoscopic, majestic, unapologetically Black visual album for *Lemonade*. I imagine searches for the term "Orisha" enjoyed quite a bump after that album and film's release. The connections have become more specific, more tangible. More easily commodified.

The Continent and the Diaspora are not the same. For Africa and African Americans, there is the added tragedy of their history's obliteration. Whites, in comprehensive fashion, sought to sever any and all connective tissue between their plunder and the land they had stolen these people from. Chattel don't have traditions.

It is among the highest order of privilege to know, with the certainty of fact, one's origins. Just as getting older teaches you the benefits of sleep that your young self enthusiastically chose to forego, so does it teach you to be curious about the past your parents experienced and those stories of theirs that annoyed you as a child. Mom used to talk of life in the village and pounding yams and I would shut my ears. Now, I beseech her for tales.

The heartbeat of privilege thumps thicker in my ears when I see how an African aesthetic has become commercialized in America, and not only embraced by Black Americans but colonized once again by whites as well. In the midst of that buying and selling lies a longing, a sense of loss that my African-American friends and colleagues always felt. That I did not have to.

There was a point in my life when, stranded between the metropole and the periphery, laden with various vectors of privilege, I figured myself the Martinician. If I was Frantz Fanon, living in Lyon, then African Americans were the Algerians, the Africans supposedly bound by cerebral and cultural defect. Then, in my sense of them as monolith, they became a peasant proletariat, a sort of pastoral ideal that seemed emblematic of America's best self. But when the specifically African-American traditions, pressurized into existence like diamonds, suddenly cycled back into mainstream culture for the consumption and enrichment of white Americans, they became true individuals, organized by class and geography and shared histories and the things that make a nation out of marksmen and mathematicians, but most evidently individuals—individuals who experienced longing or fought against it in individual fashion, who called immigrant kids in kindergarten "African booty scratcher" but grew up to name their own children after East African royalty.

Is the longing that my friends felt, in this age where so much information is so readily available to corporations and to us, a manufactured thing? Elsewhere, diasporic Africans adopt, with varying degrees of success, the mantle of their nation, even if that does not necessarily mean full assimilation. France's victorious team in the 2018 World Cup was composed almost entirely of colonial resources. Cubans, Brazilians, Jamaicans—they all have a national-cultural heritage to celebrate, and yet for so many African-Americans it can seem like a thing cobbled together: shared dialects, a shorthand forged in the foxhole, reimagined traditions that have survived near-obliteration by the forces of white supremacy. Has the longing itself been commodified?

African-American traditions are specific, and their current form resembles its precedent the same way Inuit tradition does, or Irish tradition. It is no lesser, no greater. But in America, Black cool is a profit-generating enterprise. Lips and hips and leg-swings and verbiage— talk and walk—are things lusted after by non-Blacks in

America and, thanks to globalization, all over the world. Adidas can thank Run-D.M.C. for its popularity in the '80s and '90s. Nike is worn by the professional athlete, but it's the bevy of Black youth all over the world that keep the company's lights on.

And then, the foundation having been carefully laid years prior, *Black Panther* bursts into multiplexes across the nation and barrels to a $1 billion global box office haul.

Wakanda

It began with the announcement of Ryan Coogler as director. My Black friends and I—immigrants, immigrants' children, and African Americans—could not stop talking about the fact that the man who had unveiled an adult Michael B. Jordan to us in the devastating *Fruitvale Station,* and who had provided the *Rocky* franchise the exact dosage of creative excellence to make a film simultaneously beautiful and challenging and fit-to-form and Black, would be stewarding to the screen our first solo Black superhero movie since Wesley Snipes prototyped trenchcoat chic in the criminally underrated *Blade* trilogy.

Then came the casting announcements. Michael B. Jordan would once again serve as the Robert DeNiro to Coogler's Scorsese. Angela Bassett would also star. Chadwick Boseman would lead. Lupita Nyong'o joined. As did Daniel Kaluuya. Forest Whitaker. Sterling K. Fucking Brown. With each name, our shrieks grew shriller. Their roles would long remain a mystery to us, but it did not matter. So choked with talent did this film seem that there was no metaphysical way for it to fail.

Then came the trailer.

And suddenly, everyone wanted to be from Wakanda.

#BlackPantherSoLit took over Twitter. A year later, when the first early screenings began, photos appeared of people in dashikis and agbadas, of lavish red-carpet unveilings in African capitals. Ryan Coogler's (and T'challa's) Ikiré Jones scarf. Dresses that seemed to invoke goddesses of yore. Beads, bracelets, all of it calling out to one corner or another of the Continent, its past and its present.

Africa had become the metropole.

A dear friend secured us both tickets to an early screening put on by Marvel, and I'd promised my publisher that I would, as much as I could, document the experience. Though it was freezing, I wore a daishiki my mother had gotten me after a recent trip to Nigeria. I watched a mind-bending, heart-rending movie, and as the credits rolled, I lay my head on my friend's shoulder and wept, murmuring over and over, "It's so beautiful."

I would see the movie several more times, at least once with family, Mom donning a Naija-cut flower-patterned dress and a bright white, flower-patterned gele.

This was it, the connection. This film, co-written and directed by an African American, celebrated Africa. Wakanda's costumes and customs and accents and artwork were a mélange of the Continent's reality. Listen, and you hear bits of South Africa. Squint, and you see swathes of Nigeria. Among its cast members were the London-born son of Ugandan immigrants (Kaluuya), a Tobago-born actor (Duke), the Mexico-born daughter of Kenyans (Nyong'o), the Iowan daughter of Zimbabwean immigrants (Gurira). This was the Afrofuturistic ideal: that elusive yet aspirational reunion of the Continent and the Diaspora.

Sure, we had to pay money to partake, but here it was. And it was so well made.

Then privilege began to show.

I was never asked directly to attest to the veracity of certain aspects of the film: the food, the music, the fight scenes—although the door was opened with our near-unanimous criticism of Forest Whitaker's accent. But I did come to recognize what Obinze referred to when he spoke of unearned respect, a hauteur that at first does not fit at all, then, before one realizes, fits quite comfortably. I was African, right? No one assumed I understood Nsibidi (how could I as it dates back to 400 BCE), but my family came from where that language had originated, southeastern Nigeria. I couldn't hold onto a proper Nigerian accent for too long, but I could mimic M'Baku's boisterous and assertive charm better than most of my mates. And when Daniel Kaluuya and Laetitia Wright agree to imitate each other's parents to demonstrate typical African parentage, Laetitia launches into Kaluuya's British accent to gush over his "recent" Oscar nomination for *Get Out*, to which Kaluuya, imitating his mother, responds, "…and so what? How can we convert it into jobs?"[12] Some of us laughed harder than others. As the America-bred progeny of Africa-born parents, we recognized ourselves.

And just a little bit, the equilibrium shifts. A fissure grows in the earth. A bit of Black cool branches off and circles back to African cool, America's gaze focused with heightened intensity on the Continent. *Black Panther* turned heads our way. Suddenly, African is different. Purer. "We know where we come from." And it sounds so hateful to say. But it feels of the same genre as Obinze ruminating on America's lack of luster once he realized how easily it could be arrived at with enough money.

Ifemelu, soon after her return, believes it a privilege that she has a choice, that she can always return to America. Sure, it would represent a failure of sorts, the corruption that leaves bitterness on the tongue of whoever whispers the word *Americanah*, wielding it almost like an insult. America is comfort, familiarity, ease. Still, you can't unstir a latte. Hot and cold water come together to make warm. The world gets flatter and flatter. And cool moves from America to Africa.

My privilege, I realized with no small amount of irony, lay in having the luxury to go back to Africa, should I choose to.

In October 2018, for the first time in 20 years, I returned to the country where I'd buried my father. The country that had given me my parents and our history and our cuisine and their accents and their belief in our excellence and my hot blood and their civil war scars and their love of us.

I went back to Nigeria.

PART 6

GARDEN OF EDEN

As the plane glides onto the runway at Murtala Muhammed International Airport, panic seizes my lungs. There's so much green in Ikeja outside my window. The accents and the movement of the passengers have changed. Back in Heathrow, everyone spoke English and moved with stiffness and an occasional passive-aggressive rudeness. Now, accents have thickened, people move without apology, and the air is filled with Igbo, with people standing in aisles before they are supposed to, the glorious chaos of Nigerians. I look like them, but how will I sound when I open my mouth? I haven't been working on my Naija accent. I can't pretend to be British. Not for long. Suddenly, being American feels like a deficiency. A source of shame.

My inexperience followed me through the airport and down to Customs where I overpaid my first bribe before getting to the office where I attained my visa. Beside me was another Nigerian author, Chibundu Onuzo, whose accent rang musically when she complained to the officials about the length of their process. She was here for the same festival as me. We exchanged smiles and sweated it out together in humid, un-air-conditioned annoyance. That was what did it. The complaining. The commiserating. The laughing. At that moment, Nigeria, like an older sibling who plays too rough, had opened its arms and welcomed me back.

In 2017, my debut young adult novel *Beasts Made of Night* was published. A big element of the hype in the lead-up to its launch centered on the fact that it was "Nigeria-inspired," that is to say distinctly African— that it would sit on shelves in bright and ankara-print contrast to the second-world fantasies based on Western Europe that had long since dominated bookshelves. *Black Panther*, having opened doors for a number of creators of color, was subsequently strapped onto every description of the book, which was easy marketing, even though there was nothing Afrofuturist about a novel set in a world where people wore sandals in dirt roads and worked mines with crude picks and axes and fought shadow-beasts with daggers made of simple obsidian. But it had gotten me a starred review in Kirkus and praise in NPR and a nomination for the Ilube Nommo Award for Best Speculative Fiction Novel, handed out by the African Speculative Fiction Society. My first editor had pushed me into making the story more specifically Nigerian, making it more specifically mine, and it is the best and most consequential editorial note I've ever received. Without knowing, she put me on the path to that nomination and, following that, an invitation to the Ake Arts & Book Festival, held in Lagos, and at which the award ceremony would take place.

The very next morning, the first day of the festival, we had breakfast in the hotel, buffet style. I peeled back the first of the dish covers to find white rice in one container, tomato stew in another, egusi soup in another, fried yams in yet another, and it continued and continued. Novelists and artists and filmmakers and poets slowly streamed in and we colonized tables. Before long, the place was all noise and laughter. I looked around and every single face was gorgeous. My heart trip-hammered in my chest; I fell madly in love at least five times. British-Ugandan, Zimbabwean, Nigerian by way of New York, Ghanaian, Kenyan, all gathered under one roof.

In the days to follow, I would listen to them talk about (and find myself suddenly talking about) Afropolitanism, literary traditions, gender inequality throughout the Continent, my Igbo heritage; on another panel, a historian, a novelist, a journalist, and a musician would bring their minds together to give the audience the type of multi-dimensionality needed to understand the complexity of post-Brexit racism. That first night ended in a musical extravaganza, and by the end, I, rusty and much out of practice, was out of my seat and, in a charmed bit of cultural exchange, found myself milly-rocking with Nigerian TV anchor Arit Okpo.

One day, Ugandan novelist and short story writer Jennifer Makumbi and I found ourselves talking animatedly and emotionally about children of the diaspora who find themselves, through no choice of their own, married and assimilated away from a continent they have a reawakened desire to connect with. Where does their Africanness go? Is it a finite thing to be diluted? Would they be refused because of their lack of accent, the fact that their Danish may be better than their Swahili? One late afternoon, over an early dinner, Egyptian-American journalist and author Mona Eltahawy explained the tattoos on her arms and told me the story behind her red hair and we talked about Egypt and rebellion and repression. Panashe Chigumadzi, on a panel, ribbed the Nigerians in the audience on their particular brand of imperialism, noting, quite fairly, that often when non-Africans said "Africa" or "African," they meant Nigerian. We took the dart with a boisterous, proud, understanding laugh.

The night of the concert, Salawa Abeni, the Queen of Waka Music, performed, and, with a start, I realized that nearly all of the people propelled out of their seats by her voice were the older women. They moved and sang along and pulled reluctant partners into the aisles and crowded the stage and laughed and wept and were joyous together, and I wondered if Mom had ever put in a tape or put on a vinyl recording of this woman from Ogun State and closed her eyes and vibed.

It earthquakes my heart to think even glancingly of that night.

* * *

I was ensconced in the festival grounds. We were in Lagos, but not *in* Lagos, that city so filled to bursting with greed and charity, with anger and joy, with people living life in nine dimensions. We existed in a bubble, an Edenic ideal, what Wakanda's arts and culture scene might have looked like. It was truly extraordinary.

I'd been in Black creative spaces before in the United States: workshops or brunches or Google Hangouts. We'd written and we'd talked shop and we'd commiserated and we'd learned from each other and we'd hoped and we'd dreamed and we'd sorrowed. We'd been. But in every Black space in America, creative or otherwise, hangs the threat of white violence. A gunman walking into a church. A network executive cancelling a TV show. There's always going to be a white person to walk in and ruin the whole thing.

Just before dinner, in a tented-off area near the Ouida Books bookstore that had just opened, we watched Wanjiru Kamuyu perform an interpretive dance, and I couldn't look away. Afterwards, as we inhaled what we had on our plates, I looked around and saw it. There was no white person to ruin this. Shangri-La was real.

* * *

Award-winning Nigerian-American writer and personal hero Nnedi Okorafor and I were scheduled for a book chat the afternoon of the final day of the festival. After our morning panels and before lunch, we'd been taken aside by one of the documentary filmmakers and historian and academic Louisa Egbunike. I'd recently announced a two-book deal with Penguin Random

House's Razorbill imprint, the first book about two girls trying to survive a futuristic version of the Nigerian Civil War. Dr. Egbunike was working on a project specifically about the Biafran War. Dr. Okorafor and I belonged to a generation whose parents had lived through the war. My mother was a child, her parents were slightly older. But we knew what it was like to grow up in a land foreign to this older generation, not knowing to ask, then being rebuffed when we did ask. And now we were taking the telling of that history into our own hands. Telling the history of our heritage, even those parts that were forbidden. It was the first time I'd spoken at length about the new book. It was the first time I'd spoken about the book specifically to a non-white audience.

It is a wondrous thing to grow up the child of Black immigrants in predominantly white environments, strive to understand your particular strand of Blackness, then to fellowship with others and find whiteness— ever-present whiteness—de-centered.

Nowhere has felt closer to paradise than that week in Lagos.

EPILOGUE

Only as an adult have I realized how Mom's immigrant status had positioned her while she watched the paroxysms of America's Brobdingnagian battle with its Original Sin. The War on Drugs, the Moral Majority, Rodney King and the ensuing uprising, the OJ verdict, mass incarceration, the election of Barack Obama, the election of Donald Trump—this, too, is my inheritance, to always be a step removed. I was not wounded as they were wounded. Though I am just as prey to structural racism as they, though the police state will see no difference between me and my friend who can trace their family generations back to a plantation in Georgia, though the term *nigger* does not differentiate between the first-generation Black person and the eighth-generation Black person, their wounds are not mine. It would be a lie to claim them.

We share a future, however. And this is why my uncles, with their particular political proclivities, disappoint and disturb in equal measure. They believe having been apart in the past means they will remain apart in the future, that they will brook different consideration in the eyes of lawmakers and bankers who bestow homeownership loans and the parents of the children their own children go to school with. Only a step or two removed from Frantz Fanon's *mimic men*, a caricature of white power.

So, I find myself staring down the crossroads at two diverging paths. On the one hand lies the aspirational trek towards whiteness, that asymptotic journey that promises assimilation and full acceptance at the cost of everything else, that makes of the Nigerian predilection for educational excellence an ingredient for the Model Minority myth. I see on that pathway my uncles who voted for Trump. A crowd of others who choose to vilify African Americans. Along the other path, I see my Yale classmates, immigrant creators from all over the Diaspora, my sisters. All of them leaning into their identities as Black Americans, hugging America to their chest, claiming it. And in the midst of that crowd, I see my mother, gele wrapped bright around her head, glowing like something not of this earth.

During a conversation with a journalist I met in Lagos, she'd called me a bridge. I'd told her of my Biafra novel, and she noted I'd be telling Nigerian history to a white audience, albeit a part of Nigeria precious few Nigerians themselves spoke about. I was indisputably American; I had adopted the rage of African Americans at what had been and was being done to them. But I knew where I came from.

Dr. Okorafor and I groused about the ubiquity of the term Afrofuturism after *Black Panther*'s mammoth release, how white gatekeepers and tastemakers slapped it like a badge onto any and everything. She had come up with the term Africanfuturism to describe her own work and that of other writers of science fiction from the Continent, writers whose work had been almost comprehensively shut out of American markets. Afro-futurism, a specifically American invention, blotted out their history, their efforts. And it turned an infinitely diverse continent into a single country, the objective against which the whole African literary project had spent so much of its existence fighting. Her novella, *Binti*, was Africanfuturist. So was my Biafra novel. Africa was not an imagined Promised Land whose legs were Togolese, whose left arm was Nigerian, and whose right was Ethiopian. The Africa in our novels is specific, concrete. Tangible. Realized.

Afrofuturism still has a place. Where before African-American and African discourse, dialogue, and aesthetic back-and-forth may have seemed like two ships passing in the dark, we are now close enough to touch. The Diaspora and the Continent may stand on opposite ends of the bridge, but they can see each other's luminous smiles. That's what they're doing. Smiling.

ENDNOTES

Part 1

1 Du Bois, William Edward Burghardt, and Manning Marable. *Souls of Black Folk*. Routledge, 2015, pg. 8

2 *Ibid.*, pg. 8

3 Goveia, "New Shibboleths for Old", *Caribbean Quarterly* 10: 2, June 1964, pp. 48–54; republished in *New Beacon Reviews*, Collection One, ed. John La Rose, 1968, pp. 31–7

4 Wilson Harris, as cited in Anne Walmsley, *The Caribbean Artists Movement 1966–1972: a Literary and Cultural History*, London, 1992, p. 215.

5 Du Bois, *Souls of Black Folk*, pg. 10

6 *Ibid.*, pg. 10

7 Adichie, Chimamanda Ngozi. *Americanah*. Anchor Books, 2013. pg. 5

8 *Ibid.*, pg. 8

9 *Ibid.*, pg. 135

10 *Ibid.*, pg. 136

11 *Ibid.*, pg. 137

12 *Ibid.*, pg. 137

13 *Ibid.*, pg. 207

14 *Ibid.*, pg. 207

15 *Ibid.*, pg. 207

16 *Ibid.*, pg. 174

17 *Ibid.*, pg. 174

Part 2

1 *Americanah*, pg. 166

2 *Ibid.*, pgs. 166-167

3 *Ibid.*, pg. 168

4 King Jr, Martin Luther. "Letter from Birmingham Jail."

5 *Americanah*, pg. 168

6 *Ibid.*, pg. 169

7 Stewart, Maria Miller. "Religion and the pure principles of morality, the sure foundation on which we must build." *Maria W. Stewart: America's First Black Woman Political Writer* (1995): 27–42.

8 Walker, David. "Walker's Appeal, in Four Articles; Together with a Preamble, to the Coloured Citizens of the World but in Particular, and Very Expressly, to Those of the United States of America, Written in Boston, State of Massachusetts, September 28, 1829 (Boston, 1830)." (1830), pg. 69.

9 Khalidi, Rashid. *Palestinian Identity: The Construction of Modern National Consciousness*. New York: Columbia University Press, 1997. p.194

10 Peteet, Julie. *Landscape of Hope and Despair: Palestinian Refugee Camps*. Philadelphia: University of Pennsylvania Press, 2005. p.144

11 Fanon, Frantz. *Alienation and Freedom*, ed. Jean Khalfa and Robert J. C. Young. trans. Steven Corcoran. London: Bloomsbury Academic, 2018, pg. 173

12 *Ibid.*, pg. 201

13 Fanon, Frantz. *Black Skin, White Masks*, trans. Richard Philcox. Grove Press, 2008, pg. 91, citations omitted.

14 Items taken from Fanon, Frantz. *The wretched of the earth*, trans. Richard Philcox. Grove/Atlantic, Inc., 2007, pgs. 254-277.

15 Fanon, Frantz. *Toward the African Revolution*, trans. Haakon Chevalier. Grove Press, 1994, pg. 17

16 *Ibid.*, pg. 17

17 *Ibid.*, pg. 20

18 *Ibid.*, pg. 97

19 Paraphrasing *Black Skin, White Masks*, pg. 93

20 Mehri, Momtaza, "On M.I.A." *Granta 144 Genericlovestory*, Summer 2018.

21 Baldwin, James, et al. "The negro in American culture." *Cross-Currents* 11.3 (1961): 205–224. Also available on YouTube, "The Negro in American Culture" a group discussion (Baldwin, Hughes, Hansberry, Capouya, Kazin)" at https://youtu.be/jNpitdJSXWY

22 *Ibid.*, pgs. 206

Part 3

1 *Americanah*, pg. 235

2 *Ibid.*, pg. 235

3 *Ibid.*, pg. 235

4 *Ibid.*, pg. 235

5 Wynter, Sylvia. "Unsettling the Coloniality of Being/Power/Truth/Freedom: Towards the Human, After Man, Its Overrepresentation—An Argument." *CR: The New Centennial Review*, vol. 3, no. 3, 2003, pg. 264

6 *Black Skin, White Masks*, pg. 48

7 From "President Obama Marks the 50th Anniversary of the Marches from Selma to Montgomery" (VIDEO), available at https://obamawhitehouse.archives.gov/blog/2015/03/08/president-obama-marks-50th-anniversary-marches-selma-montgomery

Part 4

1 *Americanah*, pg. 360

2 *Ibid.*, pg. 359

3 *Ibid.*, pg. 359
4 *Ibid.*, pg. 364
5 *Ibid.*, pg. 365
6 *Ibid.*, pg. 366
7 *Ibid.*, pg. 366
8 *Ibid.*, pg. 437
9 *Ibid.*, pg. 438
10 *Ibid.*, pg. 447
11 *Ibid.*, pg. 447
12 *Ibid.*, pg. 447

Part 5

1 *Americanah*, pg. 506
2 *Ibid.*, pg. 480
3 *Ibid.*, pg. 480
4 *Ibid.*, pg. 481
5 *Ibid.*, pg. 518
6 *Ibid.*, pg. 519
7 *Ibid.*, pg. 520
8 *Ibid.*, pg. 533
9 *Ibid.*, pgs. 535-536
10 *Ibid.*, pg. 553
11 "All Writing Is Political: A Conversation with Mohsin Hamid," *The Rumpus*, May 17, 2017, available at https://therumpus.net/2017/05/all-writing-is-political-a-conversation-with-mohsin-hamid/
12 Paraphrasing from "Black Panther cast on faith and parents' reactions to acting careers" [VIDEO INTERVIEW], available at https://www.youtube.com/watch?v=t5Q-VWT6ZvQ

ACKNOWLEDGMENTS

On July 12, 2018, my dear friend Madiba sent me a tweet soliciting pieces of approximately 30,000 words in length that were to serve as critical analysis for select works of fiction. I replied to the tweet with what I hoped was the picture of decorum and restraint and so began a conversation that resulted in the work before you now. Thus, my eternal thanks to Madiba for what she started and to my publisher and editor Brian Hurley for saying yes to my ideas on how I might discuss and contextualize Chimamanda Ngozi Adichie's *Americanah*. As ever, my thanks to my agent Noah Ballard who encouraged me to take this ride at full speed and who has never let caution slow down my pursuit, however reckless, of an opportunity to talk about a thing I like. I am grateful for the scholars and poets and essayists and novelists and songwriters and comic book artists who have informed the construction of this book, many of whom are enumerated in the *Notes*. Most importantly, I must acknowledge and thank my mother who has lived and continues to live a life infinitely more fascinating and variegated than my own and from whom I will never cease learning.

ABOUT THE AUTHOR

Tochi Onyebuchi is the author of *Riot Baby*, *Beasts Made of Night*, *Crown of Thunder*, *War Girls*, and *Rebel Sisters*. He has earned degrees from Yale University, New York University's Tisch School of the Arts, Columbia Law School, and L'institut d'études politiques with a Master's degree in Global Business Law.